Living by Grace

How the truth of the gospel frees
us from legalism to live the life
we were meant to live!

Reflections from
the Book of Galatians

Okezie Ofoegbu

Living by Grace

Published by
Inscript Publishing
a division of Dove Christian Publishers
P.O. Box 611
Bladensburg, MD 20710-0611
www.inscriptpublishing.com

Copyright © 2021 by Okezie Ofoegbu

Cover Design by Mark Yearnings

All rights reserved. No part of this publication may be used or reproduced without permission of the publisher, except for brief quotes for scholarly use, reviews or articles.

Scriptures marked (NIV) are from the Holy Bible, New International Version®, NIV® Copyright ©1973, 1978, 1984, 2011 by Biblica, Inc.® Used by permission. All rights reserved worldwide.

Scriptures marked (NKJV) taken from the New King James Version®. Copyright © 1982 by Thomas Nelson. Used by permission. All rights reserved.

Scriptures marked (KJVS) are taken from the King James Version of the Bible. Public Domain.

Scriptures marked (NASB) are from the New American Standard Bible®, Copyright © 1960, 1971, 1977, 1995, 2020 by The Lockman Foundation. All rights reserved.

ISBN: 9781732112537

Printed in the United States of America

Dedication

To my late Mom, Margaret Okechukwu Ofoegbu – your life, passion and love for Jesus was what God used to give me a solid foundation in His word and to show me how and what it means to live by God's grace.

Contents

Dedication	v
PREFACE	1
FOREWORD	6
CHAPTER 1	9
The News That Is Nearly Too Good to Be True	9
CHAPTER 2	22
Jesus Plus Nothing	22
CHAPTER 3	34
The Truth of the Gospel	34
CHAPTER 4	51
Obeying the Truth of the Gospel	51
CHAPTER 5	65
Living in the Flesh versus Living in the Spirit	65
CHAPTER 6	81
Faith in A Faithful God	81
CHAPTER 7	90
Our Adoption as Sons And Daughters	90
CHAPTER 8	100
The Lawful Use of the Law	100
CHAPTER 9	115
Dismantling Your Idols	115
CHAPTER 10	124
Walk in the Spirit	124
CHAPTER 11	137
From Nothing to Something	137
CHAPTER 12	150
Sustaining the Life of Grace	150

PREFACE

Living by Grace is a book that seeks to make practical a core tenet of the Christian faith: that we live by the same grace by which we are saved. The book you hold in your hand is filled with practical ways by which anyone who has received salvation by grace will also live and grow through the grace by which they are saved. Far from being just a theological treatise, it is written from a pastor's heart with practical tips to help the believer in Christ discover exactly how to live the life God always wanted humanity to live: a life lived from the glorious abundance of God's grace to humanity.

One of the most explosive things that can happen to a Christian is when they truly and fully realize that their salvation is 100% due to what God has done. However, fully realizing this throws up so many questions for the genuine seeker of God. If I have been saved, not by confidence (faith) in what I do or fail to do, but by confidence (faith) in what God has done and is doing (i.e., God's grace), what then do I do with all the laws and regulations found in the Bible and in various Christian denominations? Is the Law (such as the list of rules and regulations given by God through Moses to Israel) still required? What is the implication of breaking the Law for a Christian? If the Law is now expired or no longer relevant for righteous living, where then does my motivation for righteous living come from? Yet, how can I be saved by grace and then live by Law? How can a Law which could not give me salvation preserve a salvation it did not give? Am I saved so that I am now able to keep the Law? If so, why do I need to keep a Law that does not save? If I should, how do I keep a Law I could never keep? If I shouldn't, then what is the purpose of the law? What does it really mean to be saved by grace? Saved from what? And if I have been saved by grace, how then do I live? By grace? Or by the Law? And what does it mean "to live by grace"?

These, and many more, are the practical questions a fair-minded Christian is faced with as he or she gets introduced to the message of the gospel of grace. I was already in my 20th year as Christian when I got introduced to the gospel of God's grace. As a fairly mature Christian raised in a fairly legalistic and traditional Pentecostal/Charismatic Christian culture, these questions haunted me and contributed to my initial struggle with fully embracing the message of grace. I subsequently sought for materials to help me navigate these questions but found very few well-written and practical material out there. It was sometime in 2009/2010 when our church did a bible study on the book of Galatians that I came to discover that several of these questions troubling us in the 21st century also troubled the 1st century Christians, especially those who were gentile believers. The Apostle Paul, in writing the letter to the Galatian church, shared powerful principles to address these questions raised by the experience of these early gentile Christian believers. This book contains 12 reflections from the book of Galatians distilling

PREFACE

these principles in a straightforward and practical manner for today's believer.

In this book, you will learn that grace was always how God intended for man to live. Right there from the garden of Eden, grace was operational. You will learn also that just like in the garden, men today and throughout history are presented with a choice: to either choose to live by grace or to choose to live by law (the tree of the knowledge of good and evil). You will see how and why God warned man that if he chose to live by law, even though it was God who gave the law, man would die. You will understand why living by the law results in death and how today many believers having been saved by grace are experiencing death because they are choosing to live by law. This book will show you why humanity has experienced death and destruction and every evil imaginable since Adam (and mankind since Adam) choose and continue to choose to live by law.

But something else this book will show you is the grace of God, the fact that God, because of His love for us, did not leave man without hope and a means of salvation. God came to man in the form of Jesus, and through what God did for man, to man and in man without contribution from man (grace), God revealed to us not only how we can be delivered from legalism (the law) and all its evil consequences but also live the life God always intended us to live - under the abundant life of God's grace. This book will give you not just an understanding of what it means to be saved by grace, but, in giving practical steps and guidelines on how to live by grace, will enable you to overpower the strong temptation to revert to legalism as a way of life. No more will you be confused and burdened by fruitless attempts to hold on to and maintain your salvation by attempting to keep a Law that could not save you in the first place. Now you will learn how to be saved by grace, remain saved by grace, and grow in grace to live the life God always intended for you to live.

These reflections began as a Whatsapp chat in the Whatsapp alumni group of *God Is Love Community*, the Charismatic student group I belonged to and had the privilege of pastoring as a student between 1994 and 1997. I want to thank my General Overseer, Dr. Cosmas Ilechukwu and his wife, Dr. Deola Ilechukwu. It was their spiritual leadership, clarity of passion, and conviction of teaching that introduced me to an understanding of the grace gospel. I also owe a debt of gratitude to ministers and teachers such as Andrew Wommack, Joseph Prince, and Bill Johnson, all of whom have produced teaching that has helped clarify my understanding of the gospel of grace. Special mention must be made of Dr. Tim Keller. It was the Bible study curriculum he produced on the book of Galatians that we used in our church that helped me understand how to read this book in order to derive the benefits.

Several friends and members of my church family were instrumental in finally having this book published. A special thank you goes to several individuals whose financial support and encouragement helped ensure that this book saw the light of day. Special mention must also be made of Dr. Emmanuel Akinboye, my friend and brother in Christ, for persisting that I must write this book, including giving me ideas on how it could be published. Special thanks also go to many current and past members of my church family,

Grace Life Center Charismatic Renewal Ministries, Laurel, Maryland. That church has been crucible where I have personally tested and practiced living by grace.

Finally, I want to say a big thank you to my late mom, Mrs. Margaret Okechuwu, to whom this book is dedicated. She not only introduced me to the Christian faith, but also introduced me to reading the Bible for myself and instilled in me a hunger for the word of God that has ultimately led me to discover that staying hungry is the key to being satisfied by the abundance of what is available to us in grace. My prayer for everyone who picks this book and reads it is that a fresh hunger will be born in you for the things of God, and through this hunger, you will become satisfied as you learn to live by grace, stepping out of legalism into living the life God always intended for us to live. In Jesus Name, Amen.

Okezie Ofoegbu

FOREWORD

If the book of Romans, which is Paul's inspired thesis on the doctrine of justification, is considered his *magnum opus*, his equally inspired letter to the Galatians, easily serves as his clearest and most definitive statement on the nature of the gospel of Christ – its content, meaning and essence. Paul was firm in his conviction that the gospel is all about the salvation God has graciously provided for all peoples in all ages irrespective of their nationalities, which is assessed strictly by faith alone, in Christ and His finished work of redemption alone. This salvation is so comprehensive that it makes no allowance for any human contribution or detraction. Any human attempt to improve on or detract from it is tantamount to its repudiation. It is all of God from its conception to its consummation.

Paul claims that the gospel he preached to the Galatians was not from any human source but from Christ Himself. He explained, *"But I make known to you, brethren, that the gospel which was preached by me is not according to man. For I neither received it from man, nor was I taught it, but it came through the revelation of Jesus Christ" (Galatians 1:11-12, NKJV).* This gospel, that salvation is by grace alone through faith alone in Christ alone, without the work of the law was the same that God preached to Abraham. *"And the Scripture, foreseeing that God would justify the Gentiles by faith, preached the gospel to Abraham beforehand, saying, "In you all the nations shall be blessed. So, then those who are of faith are blessed with believing Abraham" (Galatians 3:8-9, NKJV).* Paul argued that Abraham did not attain to justification by the works he did or by obeying the law, but only by believing the promise of God. *"Just as Abraham "believed God, and it was accounted to him for righteousness." (Galatians 3:6),* so shall it be that those who will believe the gospel and place their faith in Christ will also be counted righteous in the sight of God.

When the Galatians heard this gracious gospel, which the author described as "News nearly too good to be believed," they received it with joy and relished its liberating effect. However, this freedom did not last too long before some Jewish Christian evangelists came to eclipse their euphoria in their newfound freedom by insisting that Gentile Christians must be circumcised according to the Jewish law before they could be truly saved. Paul wrote this letter as an uncompromising rebuttal of the corrupted gospel being peddled by the Judaizers. His anger and utter unwillingness to negotiate the gospel are very evident in the tone of his writing. In no other of his letters did he display this level of holy anger in correcting an error. The reason is obvious – a misleading gospel will never lead us to God. To this end, he charged his hearer, *"Stand fast therefore in the liberty by which Christ has made us free, and do not be entangled again with a yoke of bondage" (Galatians 5:1, NKJV).* The bondage in reference here is that which offers salvation as a reward of obeying the law and not as a free gift from God to be received by faith just like Abraham had modeled.

In this seminal contribution to the gospel literature, Pastor Okezie has painstakingly represented the crux of the pure gospel for the modern reader. The gospel is a message about the person and work of Jesus Christ and how His work is appropriated by faith alone. This was the bone of contention in the days of Reformation and still remains a contentious issue until now. Humanity still struggles with the pride of acknowledging that salvation is accomplished exclusively by what God alone does without any human contribution. *Living By Grace* comes with a timely message of a timeless relevance. It is a distinct call on the church to rediscover the true gospel and preach it uncompromisingly to the world that is gasping for some fresh air of God's unconditional love.

I am very happy to recommend this book to you for your pleasurable reading both for personal edification and for didactic purposes. The thoughts are coherent and logically presented, the content is thoughtful and biblically balanced, and the style is elegant and easy to read. Enjoy the read and pass it on.

Cosmas Ilechukwu.
General Overseer
Charismatic Renewal Ministries, Inc.

CHAPTER 1

The News That Is Nearly Too Good to Be True

Paul, an apostle, (not of men, neither by man, but by Jesus Christ, and God the Father, who raised him from the dead;) And all the brethren which are with me, unto the churches of Galatia: Grace be to you and peace from God the Father, and from our Lord Jesus Christ, Who gave himself for our sins, that he might deliver us from this present evil world, according to the will of God and our Father: To whom be glory for ever and ever. Amen (Galatians 1:1–5 KJVS).

When reading the Bible, understanding the historical context is very helpful and important. This approach will be valuable as we reflect on the epistle of Galatians in this book. After Paul and Barnabas were commissioned by the Church of Antioch in Acts 13, they traveled to about four or five cities in modern-day Turkey, which was then known as Galatia. These were Gentile, pagan cities, some with primitive, barbaric cultures under Roman rule at the time Paul and Barnabas arrived there. These Gentile pagans warmly received the gospel message Paul and Barnabas preached. God, working through Paul and Barnabas, baptized them with the same Holy Spirit that He gave the Jewish believers on the day of Pentecost. The Roman proconsul of the region, Sergius Paulus, was one of their first converts. He converted to Christianity following the power struggle between Paul and an influential sorcerer who had great persuasive powers over the proconsul. As a result of the efforts of Paul and Barnabas, these Gentile disciples began to organize themselves to meet in one another's homes. Churches grew in these cities.

In contrast to those who became followers of Jesus in Acts 2 through Acts 12, this was the first time non-Jews became Jesus' disciples. The revival described in Acts 13-14 brought into the Christian church people who the Jewish Christians considered idol-worshipping pagans. Many of these newly converted Gentiles were considered utterly depraved and immoral. They worshipped Greek gods such as Zeus and Hermes and their Roman counterparts. They had no relationship with any of the laws of Moses written in the Jewish scriptures. How could such people dare to begin to call themselves believers or Christians or disciples of Jesus?

> **The gospel is a news that is nearly too good to be true.**

But Luke, the author of the Acts of the Apostles and inspired by the Holy Spirit, called them believers and disciples. In Acts 13 and 14, Luke gives an eyewitness account of how Paul and Barnabas convinced these pagans to become followers of Jesus, and as a result, become saved. They were disciples indeed. These uncircumcised Gentile pagans received the baptism of the Holy Spirit. These things happened without the adoption of or compliance to any of Moses' laws by these pagans. Can you imagine how the mainstream members of the Christian church in Jerusalem, all of whom were formerly Jews or Jewish proselytes, received this news? How can a holy God give His Holy Spirit to uncircumcised and unholy perverts and pagan idol worshippers?

Perhaps the best way to appreciate these events is to imagine that you received news that people whom you considered sexual perverts and bank robbers have opened a branch of your denomination in San Francisco or gamblers and mobsters in Las Vegas. Many of us, based on our understanding of the gospel would be scandalized if such a thing happened in our churches. Which leads us to the question: exactly what gospel did Paul and Barnabas preach to these Gentiles? Exactly what did they believe so that the Holy Spirit began to call them disciples? What gospel was Paul referring to when he said, "...*the gospel we have preached unto you,*" as he wrote to believers in Galatians 1:8? What gospel produced this great result?

Fortunately, the Holy Spirit recorded for us a good summary of the exact sermon Paul preached in Antioch of Pisidia, one of the cities of Galatia. It is recorded in Acts 13:16–41:

Standing up, Paul motioned with his hand and said: "Fellow Israelites and you Gentiles who worship God, listen to me! The God of the people of Israel chose our ancestors; he made the people prosper during their stay in Egypt; with mighty power he led them out of that country; for about forty years he endured their conduct in the wilderness; and he overthrew seven nations in Canaan, giving their land to his people as their inheritance. All this took about four hundred and fifty years."

After this, God gave them judges until the time of Samuel the prophet. Then the people asked for a king, and he gave them Saul son of Kish, of the tribe of Benjamin, who ruled forty years. After removing Saul, he made David their king. God testified concerning him: 'I have found David the son of Jesse, a man after my own heart; he will do everything I want him to do.'

"From this man's descendants, God has brought to Israel the Savior Jesus, as he promised. Before the coming of Jesus, John preached repentance and baptism to all the people of Israel. As John was completing his work, he said: 'Who do you suppose I am? I am not the one you are looking for. But there is one coming after me whose sandals I am not worthy to untie.'

"Fellow children of Abraham and you God-fearing Gentiles, it is to us that this message of salvation has been sent. The people of Jerusalem and their rulers did not recognize Jesus, yet in condemning him, they fulfilled the words of the prophets that are read every Sabbath. Though they found no proper ground for a death sentence, they asked Pilate to have him executed. When they had carried out all that was written about him, they took him down from the cross and laid him in a tomb. But God raised him from the dead, and for many days he was seen by those who had traveled with him from Galilee to Jerusalem. They are now his witnesses to our people.

"We tell you the good news: What God promised our ancestors he has fulfilled for us, their children, by raising up Jesus. As it is written in the second Psalm:

The News That Is Nearly Too Good to Be True

"You are my Son; today I have become your Father.'

God raised him from the dead so that he will never be subject to decay. As God has said,

"'I will give you the holy and sure blessings promised to David.'

So it is also stated elsewhere:

"You will not let your holy one see decay.'

"Now when David had served God's purpose in his own generation, he fell asleep; he was buried with his ancestors and his body decayed. But the one whom God raised from the dead did not see decay.

"Therefore, my friends, I want you to know that through Jesus the forgiveness of sins is proclaimed to you. Through him everyone who believes is set free from every sin, a justification you were not able to obtain under the Law of Moses. Take care that what the prophets have said does not happen to you: "

'Look, you scoffers, wonder and perish, for I am going to do something in your days that you would never believe, even if someone told you."

Paul's sermon is essentially a story. He is giving a historical account of the interaction between God and His people, Israel. He starts off by reminding the people that God chose their ancestors. It was not their ancestors who chose God. God chose them because He loved them, not because they loved Him (Deuteronomy 7:7–8). He chose them so that through them, God's love, light, and salvation would extend to the rest of the world. Paul, however, goes on to outline the long, topsy-turvy history of the relationship between God and His people. Paul described how, again and again, God's chosen people rejected God and, consequently, broke His law. It was as if God's chosen people could not obey Him or do His will, no matter how hard they tried. They constantly broke God's heart and failed in achieving God's hope that the world would be blessed through them. Yet, in all of this, God did not reject them or promise them destruction. Instead, he "endured their conduct" and promised to send them a Savior, a descendant of David, who would do "everything God wanted." Through this Savior, God's people would be rescued. In other words, although His people were lost through their unjust ways and deserving of death. He promised to send them a Savior, a King, someone to rescue them from their sins and the terrible effects on their lives. The Savior would do what God wanted!

Paul was preaching this message around AD 45. He says to them that he came with good news. God has indeed sent that Savior, Deliverer, and King. His name is Jesus of Nazareth. Yes, that traveling Jewish rabbi who was crucified in Jerusalem about fifteen years earlier is the Messiah. Jesus was the One who will do "everything God wants" on our behalf. Paul then made a case for how Jesus of Nazareth was indeed that King, Savior, and Deliverer. He mentions several prophecies of the Messiah that Jesus fulfilled. He refers to John the Baptist, whom many of these Jews accepted as a genuine prophet of God. As John the Baptist was wrapping up his ministry, he prophesied that Jesus was the one who was to come. Paul reminded his audience of the prophecy in Isaiah 53, where Isaiah stated that the servant of the Lord, the Messiah, would be slain for the sins of humanity, destroyed like a "lamb brought to the slaughter" (53:7). Well, that was exactly what happened to Jesus, Paul said. He pointed out to them how, even though there were no grounds for his condemnation, the Jewish rulers conspired with the Roman rulers to have him crucified. It happened just as it had been prophesied.

Paul then shared the biggest news of all: "God has raised Jesus from the dead!" It was just as David prophesied. Paul reminded them of the prophecy that said God's servant would not "see decay." Jesus, he said, had not seen decay; three days after he was buried, God raised him from the dead. Hundreds of eyewitnesses could testify to this— including Barnabas and Paul himself. Why is this point about Jesus rising from the dead, never to die again, so important? You see, Jews in Paul's time connected death to sin. People die because they sin. As Ezekiel prophesied, the soul that sins shall die (Ezekiel 18:20). Therefore, if God indeed raised Jesus from the dead, it meant God acknowledged Jesus as perfectly righteous and not deserving of death. Consequently, in line with Jewish law, here is a man who would qualify to be the unblemished Lamb of God, who could be presented in the temple to bear the sins of others and die because of their sins.

Paul makes this point: Jesus indeed is the perfect Lamb of God, by Whom and through Whom God has made the required payment for the sins of all people! Paul was saying to his audience that: *"although our lives have been one of constant* *sin and rebellion against God, God came as Jesus to taste the death **every man deserved**, and when God raised Jesus from the grave, God made everlasting life available to every man. So that now, having ascended into Heaven, His life and His Spirit has been made available to us all forever"* (Acts 13:32-34, paraphrased). God has sent Jesus as that King and Deliverer whom God promised would come and save His people from all evil. *"Be it known unto you all, therefore, that through this man Jesus, you who are full of sin, are declared forgiven"*, Paul declares (Acts 13:38-39).

> **Be it known unto you all, therefore, that through this man Jesus, you who are full of sin, are declared forgiven (Acts 13:38–39)**

In AD 45, Paul announced to these people a gospel, a news that was nearly too good to be true. He informed them that, because of what God has done through Jesus, all their sins - past, present, and future - have been forgiven. Whether they were moral Jews or immoral pagans, it did not matter. God had done it. God had unilaterally, unconditionally, and supernaturally forgiven them *all* their wrongdoings, without their even asking for it. Think about all those things the law condemned them for. In Jesus, God has declared them "justified i.e. released them from the evil consequences of their actions. Because of what God has done, it is really just as if they never sinned. Paul declared with all boldness that we

The News That Is Nearly Too Good to Be True

ALL have been accepted by God because of this man Jesus. We ALL can receive that same Spirit of God that Jesus had. Whoever you may be, it does not matter, whether you are Jew or Gentile, rich or poor, Greek or Barbarian, moral or immoral - all of us who were previously excluded because of sin are now *fully* accepted by God. And this is not because of anything *we* have done; it is 100 percent because of what Jesus did, the One who "has done all things well" (Mark 7:37). This is what Paul refers to as the "grace of God" — what God has done for us, in us, and to us, with no contribution from us. Paul tells his hearers this story and persuades them to believe in this grace of God and to continue in it (Acts 13:43). Note the words "continue in the grace of God" or "live by the grace of God." They will come up again because they are the foundation — the theme — of this book.

Let me summarize the gospel message that Paul preached to these Galatians. It must be the gospel that we hear, believe, or preach to others. I invite you to reflect on these words: **God has done *everything* required for you to be saved from your sins and all their negative consequences. Therefore, to be saved and enter God's kingdom, all you have to do is to 1) believe in what God has done for you, in you, and to you, with no contribution from you; and 2) to continue living in, and from, what God has done in you, to you, and for you.** In other words, once you believe that God has done everything to save you, you must live every day in the light of the truth of what God has done and how you have been changed as a result — even when no physical or natural evidence says it is so. The second aspect is **obeying the truth** of what God has done, or living according to the truth of the good news of God's grace. As we shall see later in this book, "obeying the truth of the gospel" is also the same thing as "walking in the Spirit," "living by faith," or "walking in God's love." That is the purpose and goal of this book: to help you live in line in line with this too-good-to-be-true news. The argument made in this book is that this is how God always intended for humans to live.

Concluding the story in Acts 13, we see that after Paul preached this sermon in a Jewish synagogue, the next weekend, almost the whole city came to hear the word of God. Think about it. Why did this happen? The deep implications of Paul's gospel inspired the people. Jesus suffered and died to rescue all people from the consequences of all their sins — past, present, and future. This means absolutely *no one* is excluded any longer from participating in God's kingdom. Before this, *only* the Jews were regarded as God's people because of their adherence to laws that Gentiles could not keep or were not interested in keeping. But now, if what Paul said was true, *everyone from every nation* was now eligible to have a relationship with God. Can you imagine the conversations people were having in their homes, workplaces, and marketplaces after Paul announced this news? Can you imagine the excitement in the city among men and women who had been burdened with years of servitude in religion? Paul's message unleashed a revival in the city. At the core of his teaching was the message that God's love has been freely extended to *all* humanity - no matter who you are. What a radical message.

Have you heard this message? Does it sound nearly too good to be true? Have you experienced the excitement that such a message brings? Have you seen yourself wholly and completely rescued from the consequences of not just your past sins but of the ones you are yet to commit? Have you experienced the exhilarating feeling of knowing that *nothing* stands between you and your Father God? Do you know that because of what Jesus did, God no longer counts your sins against you? Today, if you go into eternity without God, it would not be because of lying, cheating, sexual immorality, stealing, or murder or any sinful thing you may have done. None of those sins are being counted against you now because of what Jesus did. Rather it would be for one reason and one reason only — that you did not believe this too-good-to-be-true news and continued to live as if this too-good-to-be-true news was indeed true.

This is the good news. Not the list of things that you need to do, but the good news of *all* God has done for you in Jesus. It is this message that Paul summarized as he opened his Letter to the Galatians in Galatians 1:3–4: Jesus gave himself to rescue us from the death and the evil consequences of ALL our sins. He did this out of his unconditional love for us. Do you want to receive this life that Jesus offers? Do you want to get right with God on the basis of what God has done for you and not what you do for him? Then believe that what you have just heard is true and say this prayer from your heart:

Father, I confess that I have lived in sin and rebellion against you! I have not served you or worshipped you in Spirit and truth. Even the good works I have done are like filthy rags before you. But I also confess that by His death on the cross, in Jesus you forgave me all my sins because you love me. I also confess that when you raised Him from the dead, you offered me eternal life in Him. And so today, I accept Jesus as my Lord and my Savior. I accept His death and resurrection as the basis of my acceptance with You. I receive forgiveness of all my sins, and I receive the New Life which You have made available to all people. Jesus, come take your rightful place in my life. Come reign in my heart and fill me with Your love and Your life. Restore me, Jesus. Live in me. Love through me. Thank you, Father. I am now saved. Jesus is my Lord. Jesus is my Savior. Thank you, Father God, for forgiving me, saving me, and for giving me eternal life with You. In Jesus's name, I pray.

DEEPENING YOUR UNDERSTANDING

- What about the historical setting of the book of Galatians was new to you? What could help you gain a better understanding of the book?

- Is the description of Paul's presentation of the gospel, i.e. essentially as news or an announcement of a historical event fair? Why? Also, why do you think the gospel is not presented more in this manner today?

- The year AD 45 marked almost twenty years since the death and resurrection of Jesus and the great commission for the apostles to go into "all nations" and evangelize (Matthew 28:19). Why do you think that the apostles and the early church confined the announcement of the good news to only Jews and Gentile proselytes?

- How are our views about Christians who are different from us in tribe, background, culture, opinions, or dress styles the same as or different from what occurred in the days of the apostles?

 APPLYING WHAT YOU HAVE LEARNED

Now, what do I do?

- If it is true that Jesus is the King who God promised will come to rescue you and save you because you are unable to save yourself, what implication does that have on how you relate with Jesus?

- If the gospel is an announcement of what has been done for you, what then must you do for you to benefit from what has been done for you?

- If the grace of God means what God has done for you through Jesus, is there anything you can do to *undo* what God has done for you? Under what circumstances could what God has done for you be of no value to you?

- What can you do to "continue in grace," i.e., continue in what God has done for you through Jesus?

CHAPTER 2

Jesus Plus Nothing

I marvel that ye are so soon removed from him that called you into the grace of Christ unto another gospel: Which is not another; but there be some that trouble you, and would pervert the gospel of Christ. But though we, or an angel from heaven, preach any other gospel unto you than that which we have preached unto you, let him be accursed. As we said before, so say I now again, If any man preaches any other gospel unto you than that ye have received, let him be accursed (Galatians 1:6–9, KJVS).

As you read Paul's Letter to the Galatians, one thing that gets your attention is how upset he seemed to be. This is the one letter of Paul in the Bible in which he does not offer his usual elaborate opening greetings. Neither does he end with his effusive goodbyes. He hardly mentions any names of the brethren or families in the church. Missing are his usual words of thanksgiving, prayers, or personal affections, which he typically showered on his converts, even when they commit grievous and obnoxious sins. If you recall, Paul said the Corinthians were "called to be saints" (1 Corinthians 1:2). Paul thanked God always for the grace of God over their lives (1:4), even though he would lambaste them later for allowing in their fellowship a man who was in sexual relations with his father's wife (I Corinthians 5). He would rebuke the lazy Thessalonian brethren who refused to work in the name of being born again (2 Thessalonians 3:10), even though he greeted them by saying that he never ceases to remember their "work of faith, and labor of love, and patience of hope" (1 Thessalonians 1:3). But you see none of these in Paul's Letter to the Galatians. This is remarkable because this was the first letter Paul wrote, and indeed, the first written document by an apostle after the letter written at the end of the Council at Jerusalem in Acts 15.

Why would Paul withhold his usual and typical platitudes and greetings? What was going on with the Galatians that made Paul begin his letter with a severe attack on these brethren and the false teachers who were troubling them? Why would Paul still call believers in Corinth saints of God even though that church was troubled with sexual immorality, idol worship, infighting, and schisms? Yet he uses harsh words, such as "foolish Galatians" and "bewitched Galatians" for the brethren in Galatia. Would we call a church where sexual immorality and divisions exist "the house of God" today? Conversely, would we call a church where there are strong rules and requirements for being called a Christian "a house of witches"?

But this is what Paul essentially did. Paul was very agitated with the Galatians because they had allowed some people who were "perverting" the gospel to have sway over their lives. These men of God had come to these newly minted Gentile believers in the region of Galatia and imposed on them fairly stringent moral rules and religious regulations to live by, all of which they got from the portion of the Bible that we call the Old Testament today. They taught these new believers that they had to keep these rules in order to be saved or maintain their salvation. These pastors and teachers, rather than showing them how to "continue in the grace of Christ" as Paul and Barnabas had done, came to this church preaching a different "gospel," one that, although it started by acknowledging the grace of God to the sinner through the death of Jesus, added other things which believers must do in addition to receiving that grace.

> **Grace is what God has done to you, for you and in you with no contribution from you.**

To paraphrase, Paul does not mince words when he says, "...if anyone comes to announce to you a gospel different from what we announced to you, let him be accursed". We could also use the word *anathema*, which means "cursed with an irrevocable ecclesiastical curse" (See 1 Corinthians 16:22). In modern language, Paul is saying: "What they are telling you looks like the gospel, but it is **NOT** the gospel; instead, it is a perversion, a corruption, a poisonous counterfeit of the true gospel. The false gospel will end up harming and ruining you." From Paul's perspective, this was more dangerous to a Christian than sexual immorality, fornication, adultery, idol worship, debauchery, homosexuality, and any other vice that the pagan Christians struggled with. Paul never placed an anathema curse on anyone who practiced those sins, but he did not hesitate to do so to anyone who accepted or promoted this false gospel. What, then, was this other "gospel" being preached and announced to these Galatian Christians? Why did Paul consider it so dangerous? Why did these people succeed in confusing these young Gentile converts? Is that "gospel" still alive in our day? How can we identify this false gospel and be able to avoid it?

Let's start by recalling what the core of Paul's gospel was. Paul's nearly too good-to-be-true message is that "God has done *ALL* that is needed for men and women to be saved. Therefore, by believing and accepting as true what God has done for you in the Lord Jesus Christ, you will be saved, i.e., experience indeed your rescue from the evil consequences of your sins by God. Now, having been saved, live like one who has been saved ("continue in God's grace"), producing good works expected in the life of someone whom God has indeed rescued. We see Paul expound this gospel in many other letters he wrote to his Gentile converts. For example, here is a paraphrase of Romans 12:2:

> *"Dear brethren, <u>because of what God has done for you</u>, be transformed through the renewing of your mind. Present your bodies as a sacrifice to God. This is the only reasonable and logical way to live if you have received God's mercies."*

In Ephesians 4:1, he wrote: *"if you have been saved, live worthy of your call."* In Philippians 2:12, he enjoins believers who listened to his gospel and obeyed his command to believe in it, to now work out the salvation they have received. In all his writings, Paul never said good works are not needed.

He only says they are a fruit of who you are, not the root of who you want to be. Good works are the natural outflow of people who continue in God's grace by making every effort to live out all the good works God has *already* done in their lives.

However, we are told in Acts 15:1 that *"certain men which came down from Judaea taught the brethren, and said, Except ye be circumcised **after the manner of Moses**, ye cannot be saved."* We need to understand what was happening here to fully understand what Paul wrote in his Letter to the Galatians. Let me try to paint the picture for you as best as I can. Up until this time, *only* Jews or Gentile proselytes became believers in Jesus. Every single person who was a follower of Jesus was either a Jew who had been living under Mosaic law, a Gentile who had completely converted to Judaism (i.e. a Gentile proselyte), or a Gentile who had not fully converted but accepted the laws of Moses as the principles to govern their lives. This last group was called "devout" in the New Testament and included men like Cornelius.

The bottom line is this: until now, only "circumcised" people had converted to Christianity. So when these Jewish believers heard that "uncircumcised Gentiles" were claiming to be Christians, they were aghast. In their perspective, there was no way people who had not committed to keeping the basic rudiments of the Mosaic law could be saved. According to their logic and thinking, yes, it *is* the sacrifice of Jesus that saves. However, one cannot rule out that God sent Jesus to save them after He saw their commitment, desire, and zeal in trying to do their best to serve Him and to live according to His laws and principles. And one of the ways of showing this commitment is getting circumcised! In other words, salvation by faith in Jesus was almost like God's reward for the effort, even if a failed effort. No one can expect to be saved, they said, if they are not making any effort to keep the law of God. God essentially sends Jesus to help you when your efforts fall short.

Therefore, from the perspective of these Jewish believers, they were not against Paul's gospel—not at all! Salvation is still by faith in Jesus alone, they claimed. In fact, they claimed that what they were preaching was exactly the same gospel as Paul's. If anything, they were just making sure the Galatians got the "full" gospel, not something "watered down," which Paul may have inadvertently done in his desire for converts. So these Jewish believers, in a bid to preserve the purity and holiness of their church, came all the way from Jerusalem, saying to the Galatian Gentile believers: "We are here to present to you something that Paul may have left out from the gospel he preached to you." According to these Judaizers, while believing in Jesus was a very important step, it was not the only step toward being saved. They told them they had to keep the law, specifically the Mosaic law of circumcision, in addition to believing in the Lord Jesus, or else they **could not** be saved. In other words, their gospel message was: *Faith in what God has done for you in Jesus is necessary, but not sufficient for you to be saved; Yes, believe in the Lord Jesus, but you must live like someone who has believed (keep the laws, do good works—in this case, circumcision), and then you are saved (or remain saved).* In other words, without your effort to keep the law, in this case, by being circumcised, you cannot be saved, and your salvation is incomplete.

Part of what made this "gospel" message sound so credible was that these people came from Jerusalem, the headquarters of the church itself, and were probably very influential pastors and leaders who were very close to the apostles Peter and James. In fact, James was the brother of Jesus himself. They also claimed that James sent them. At that time, James was the bishop of the Jerusalem church. Further, as Paul would later allude, they also appeared to denigrate Paul and sowed seeds of doubt in the brethren's hearts regarding the authenticity of Paul's apostleship. They may have pointed out to these Gentile believers that Paul never saw Jesus, so his claim to apostleship was bogus. Also, he had killed Christians. Would God give such an important message to someone like that? Again, all of these seemed compelling and lined up with the gospel they peddled, i.e., *faith in Jesus – while important – was not all that was needed. One's lifestyle was important in receiving that which God had done.*

With this background, you can, therefore, appreciate why Paul had to make strong statements like *"even if it were us or an angel from heaven who comes and preaches another gospel different from the one we preached to you, let that person be cursed."* According to Paul, it was inconceivable that having been saved by faith in Jesus, that people would abandon it later and invent a method to be saved by their works. Paul's ink is, therefore, dripping with holy anger against these Jewish Christians as he tries to undo the damage these "brethren" have done to the nascent faith of these pagan converts. He calls their message toxic and dangerous. He calls it *bewitchment*. He calls it *walking after the flesh*. He calls it *falling from grace*. He says this message, which looks like the gospel –

is *not* the gospel. Why is this an important point for him to make? Because the truth of the gospel is that God does not accept us through Christ plus something we have done; he accepts us by Christ alone. Jesus plus nothing is everything. But Jesus plus something is nothing! 1 John 2:2 tells us: "*And He is the propitiation for our sins, and not for ours only, but also for the sins of the whole world.*" The word *propitiation* means "satisfaction." Jesus satisfies God. To be accepted by God, we, too, must be satisfied with what satisfies God. Paul countered these false teachers by telling the Galatians that: "*When I presented this message, Peter, James, and John confirmed that this indeed was also what Jesus had told them, too. They added nothing to me!*" (see Galatians 2:6).

Whenever someone tells you that faith in Jesus plus something you have to do is what assures, guarantees, or maintains your salvation, you must reject it vehemently. In Galatia, it was faith in Jesus plus circumcision. Later on, as we see in Colossians, they added the keeping of "holy days," of Sabbaths, abstaining from certain kinds of foods, and so on. In our day, we see it in the form of "faith in Jesus plus your holy living," and so on. But when believers ask for a definition of holy living, pastors and Bible study leaders rattle off a list of "big sins" which people have not yet been caught in, such as fornication, adultery, homosexuality, and so on. Church leaders forget that, according to James 2:10, if someone keeps the whole law and yet breaks one, they have broken all. In other words, in the eyes of the law, if someone tells a "harmless" white lie, that person is also an adulterer, a fornicator, and a homosexual! Which means if we are saved by faith in Jesus plus our "holy living"—none of us is holy enough to be saved!

Other people in the church have specific expectations on how individuals should style their hair, what type of clothes they wear, or whether clubbing and partying are acceptable. They are also concerned for those who engage in antisocial behavior. For some others, it is whether or not you wear jewelry, or other ornamentation, or the level of your commitment to church activities. I have heard people say that God punishes people with car accidents because they left ministries! Can you imagine that? Other reasons include not praying that morning or because they had unforgiveness in their hearts.

I, too, was brought up in a Christian culture that espoused teachings like this. For several years after I got saved, I was taught, and I taught others, that unless a woman covers her hair to pray, God would not hear her prayers. This teaching is foolishness and bewitchment. If it were true that God hears a woman's prayer when she covers her hair with a scarf, then Muslim women who wear hijab would have the most answered prayers. God answers our prayers, not by covering our hair, but because of what Jesus did. Because of the grace of God. Like the Judiazers in Galatia, we also proved this doctrine from the Bible. Many of us do not realize that because a doctrine is stated in the Bible that it does not make that doctrine the gospel that brings salvation. The gospel of God's grace that brings salvation is the story of what God has done to save me, to heal me, and to bless me, with no contribution from me. All I have to do is believe it to receive it. It is that salvation that produces good works in us and not vice versa.

I was also taught, and I taught others, that women should not wear pants or trousers because it was contrary to the Law of Moses. Again we felt that we were proving this doctrine from the Bible. But again, here's the problem: if God accepts you because of the type of clothing you wear, then Jesus died in vain. Why would Jesus need to die if all I needed to do was to dress in a certain way? If that were the case, the best dressed would always have the advantage over those who are not well dressed. Christianity then devolves to the nature of our wardrobes rather than the strength of the God we have believed. It wasn't until I began to understand the gospel that I began to drop many of these false teachings. It is because of what *God* did that I am saved, not because of what I did or did not do.

> **Jesus plus nothing is everything; Jesus plus something is nothing.**

Today, we see these false teachings manifest in teachings on tithes, offerings, and giving; faithfulness in church attendance, and Christian work and ministry, among others. We must be careful. Whenever, in an effort to encourage people to perform good works, it is preached that a man or woman who does not seem to be keeping the laws of God in the Bible is *not* saved (or more subtly, will not be blessed by God, or will be rejected or abandoned by God), that message is *not* the gospel. Such a gospel is a counterfeit gospel; if you hold onto such beliefs, Paul says, you are "foolish" and "bewitched." Salvation has *nothing* to do with *anything* we do. We contribute *nothing* to our salvation because we have *nothing* to contribute. All our self-righteousness is as filthy rags! The *only* reason why we are saved, the only reason why God blesses us, and the only reason why God accepts us is because of what Jesus did. Nothing we do or don't do moves God in his attitude toward us. God hears our prayers, welcomes us, accepts us, and blesses us, not because of anything we do but *because of what Jesus did.* **Jesus plus nothing is everything; Jesus plus something is nothing.** God did not send Jesus to help us in our failed attempts at holiness. No! He sent Jesus because *no one* is ever going to be holy enough.

Today, as you receive this message, let Jesus plus nothing be enough for you and satisfy you; it is enough for God and satisfies God. Let no one, not even an angel from heaven, compel you to do one more thing to add to your faith in what God did through Jesus in order for you to receive and enjoy God's eternal life.

Lay your deadly "doing" down
Down at Jesus's feet;
Stand in Him, in Him alone,
Gloriously complete.
(from the hymn "It is Finished" by James Proctor, 1864)

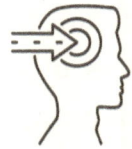

DEEPENING YOUR UNDERSTANDING

- What is the fundamental difference between the gospel message Paul announced and the gospel message as announced by the Christian Jews from Judea?
- In what practical, truth-filled ways could we today announce the gospel as the Christian Jews in Paul's

day did and not as Paul did? How could we make the gospel a "Jesus plus nothing" endeavor?

- Paul considered the Christian Jews' gospel as extremely dangerous and used the strongest words to denounce that gospel and those peddling it. What do you think was the reason for this? What makes this version of the gospel so dangerous?

- Why would the Christian Jews from Judea be genuinely skeptical about the message Paul was peddling?

APPLYING WHAT YOU HAVE LEARNED

- Quickly review your understanding of the gospel. Where do you tend to lean toward most of the time? Are you more of a "believe in the Lord Jesus and you are saved; now live like someone who is saved"? Or do you lean more toward "Believe in the Lord Jesus. Now that you believe, make sure you are living right, and then you will be saved or remain saved?"

- What can you do today to improve or increase what God has done for you through Jesus? Or to ask God to do more for you through Jesus?

- What can you do today to receive more or increase your experience of what God has done for you through Jesus?

- What can you do to make sure that *Jesus plus nothing* is the only basis of your acceptance by God?

CHAPTER 3

The Truth of the Gospel

*Then fourteen years after I went up again to Jerusalem with Barnabas, and took Titus with me also. And I went up by revelation, and communicated to them that gospel which I preach among the Gentiles, but privately to those who were of reputation, lest by any means I might run, or had run, in vain. But neither Titus, who was with me, being a Greek, was compelled to be circumcised. And that because of false brethren unawares brought in, who came in privily to spy out our liberty which we have in Christ Jesus, that they might bring us into bondage:, to whom we gave place by subjection; no, not for an hour, that the **truth of the gospel** might continue with you (Galatians 2:1–5, NKJV).*

"The truth sets you free, so you can freely live the truth" (John 8:32).

Johann Bunyan, a Puritan from the seventeenth century, wrote The Pilgrim's Progress. He was a pastor severely persecuted for his faith. He wrote *The Pilgrim's Progress* during his twelve years of incarceration. But Bunyan was not always so bold and full of faith. As a young man, soon after he became an ardent Christian, he suffered severe bouts of a guilty conscience as he struggled with his sins.

The Truth of the Gospel

In Chapter 8 of his classic work *Grace Abounding to the Chief of Sinners*, Bunyan described his experiences with these struggles. He writes:

... the tempter began afresh to mock my soul another way, saying that Christ indeed did pity my case, and was sorry for my loss: but forasmuch as I had sinned and transgressed as I had done, [Christ] could by no means help me, nor save me from what I feared; for my sin was not of the nature of theirs for whom he bled and died, neither was it counted with those that were laid to his charge when he hung on the tree; therefore, unless Christ should come down from heaven and die anew for this sin, though indeed he did greatly pity me, yet I could have no benefit of him ....

Bunyan describes the misery he felt as the devil tormented him by convincing him that, while indeed Christ's death covered the sins of others, his own sins were too great to be covered. Bunyan somehow believed that even though Jesus Christ pitied him, He could not help him. Bunyan believed that Jesus could not remain faithful to His threats against people who sinned the kind of sins Bunyan had committed and at the same time extend his mercy, even though he knew Jesus still loved and pitied him. Bunyan writes:

...so that the ground of all these fears of mine did arise from a steadfast belief I had of the stability of the holy word of God, and also from my being misinformed of the nature of my sin. But oh, how this would add to my affliction, to conceive that I should be guilty of such a sin, for which he did not die. These thoughts did so confound me, and imprison me, and tie me up from faith that I knew not what to do... but oh...how would I pray him and entreat him to count and reckon this sin among the rest for which he died.

But this scripture would strike me down as dead: "Christ being raised from the dead, dieth no more; death hath no more dominion over him."

What Bunyan describes is what I have found, in various degrees, as the experience of many Christians today. It was also my own experience for the first twenty-plus years of my Christian walk. We are confounded and confused about our relationship with God, our Father. This confusion does not come from unbelief about God or His word. On the one hand, we read the scriptures, and we see Jesus crucified for our sins, dying on the cross to cleanse us of them. We come to Him in faith and receive salvation because we understand that we can never save ourselves. Our salvation is indeed by faith in the finished work of Jesus. As the book of Genesis describes, we behold the work of the Lord, and it is good. *"And the evening and the morning were the first day" (Genesis 1:5, KJVS).*

Day Two comes along, and things are simply glorious. We wake up full of joy for what we received on Day One. We bask in the glory of the creation that we have become. Old things indeed seem to have passed away; all things are new and beautiful. Songs bubble up from our hearts. We start praying and never seem to stop. We read the Bible and it all comes alive. Wow! New life! New joy! Our joy is unspeakable and full of glory (see 1 Peter 1:8). We behold the work of the Lord in our lives and how we have lived on this day, and it is good. As Tyndale says, *"our hearts are glad and we sing, and dance and leap for joy."*

But then comes Day Three, and things begin to go haywire. It starts with a sudden lack of interest in praying and reading the word. Our spouses, children, colleagues, or friends may feel irritable for some reason and take it out on us. Defensive, we explode in anger. We thought God had dealt with these manifestations of our behavior and sins on Day One. And we thought we had conquered them on Day Two. Our lives completely go out of control from that point on. We say things that we don't mean to say. We read books and watch films and TV programs we know are bad for us. We hold deep bitterness and anger toward people. By the time we retire at the end of the day, we behold the work of our hands and the life we have lived. It is not good, but evil. And then the devil comes and whispers in our ears: *"You thought you were saved? Even if you were saved on Day One, you are clearly no longer saved on Day Three! After all, is it not written: 'we that will go back to sin willfully, there remaineth no more sacrifice for sin.' (Hebrews 10:26)?"*

As Bunyan said, it is not unbelief in God that causes you to be tormented in this way. It is faith in the word of God (or at least your understanding of that word) which produces this misery. And to this day, countless believers find themselves in the same position. Bunyan lived during the 1600s, and even then, people, because of their sins, were tossed to and fro by the torments of their consciences, endlessly praying and asking God to come again, be merciful, and save them. You may be feeling exactly that way too today. What you, and many believers like you, need is not to pray again and again to be saved. Instead, you need to come to a powerful and life-changing understanding of what Paul called in Galatians "the truth of the gospel." It is important to note this term and its various expressions in the New Testament. It is at the heart of unleashing the power of the gospel in your life.

The truths of the gospel are simply the deep implications of the gospel. They are the truths embedded in the gospel message of what God did for us in Jesus. Let me put it this way. People who live by the truth of the gospel say, "If it is true that God has done X for me, then Y has to be true in my life, even if everything around me seems to suggest that this is not the case." The fact is, when you received Jesus as your Lord and Savior, God placed you "in Christ." This is an established biblical truth. This is the X of what God has done for you. If you are truly and actually in Christ (i.e., if X is true), the Bible is then filled with hundreds of thousands of God's promises to everyone who is in Christ (the Ys). Consequently, your life as a Christian is a lifelong journey of discovering all the great things God has done to you, in you, and for you with no contribution from you "in Christ Jesus." Every day, you should meditate upon the works of God's grace, seeking to understand the implications these works of God *must* have in your life. As you discover them, you cooperate with your Father by taking advantage of all the resources God has provided to experience all that God has given you by His grace.

In 2005, God brought me into a clearer understanding of what happened to me when I received Jesus as my Lord and Savior. This is what living a life of grace, or the grace life, means. The same thing happened to John Bunyan. He writes:

> *...one day as I was passing into the field, this sentence fell upon my soul: 'Thy righteousness is in heaven.' And with the eyes of my soul, I saw Jesus at the Father's right hand. 'There,' I said, 'is my righteousness!' So that wherever I was or whatever I was doing, God could not say to me, 'Where is your righteousness?' For it is always right before him. I saw that it is not my good frame of heart that made my righteousness better, nor yet my bad frame that made my righteousness worse, for my righteousness is Christ. Now my chains fell off indeed. My temptations fled away, and I lived sweetly at peace with God. Now I could look from myself to him and could reckon that all my character was like the coins a rich man carries in his pocket when all his gold is safe in a trunk at home. Oh, I saw that my gold was indeed in a trunk at home, in Christ my Lord. Now Christ was all: my righteousness, sanctification, redemption.*

That, my friends, is the powerful "truth of the gospel," setting someone free from the endless torment of the devil's lies. For if it is true - and it *is* true - that because I am now in Jesus, Jesus is now "my righteousness," and Jesus is now in heaven at the right hand of God; then it must also be true that my righteousness is not here on earth; it is in heaven. And so, if my righteousness is *not* here on earth, what can I do here on earth to increase or diminish my righteousness? Nothing! Wow! What a life-transforming message!

Like the Jewish Christians of Paul's day, many modern Christians try to use the keeping of the law to balance the gospel message. When we do this, it is evidence of a lack of knowledge about the "truth of the gospel" concept. The gospel truth itself is balanced, and we should concern ourselves with gaining a deeper understanding of it and expounding it to others. We must learn to announce the gospel with complete clarity and boldness to humankind, for Paul says that it is the "power of God for salvation to **EVERY ONE**" (Romans 1:16), no matter how good, bad, or ugly they may be. The announcement of what God did for people in Christ two thousand years ago is what unleashes the power of God in each person's life for salvation. The power of God is not what people do today, two thousand years after God has *finished* the work. To those people, I say along with Jesus: "Do not fear, but only believe" (Mark 5:36). Then they would have life-changing encounters with the power of God.

> The power of God is not in what people do today. The power of God is in what God has done through Jesus two thousand years ago.

I remember the day in 2006 when a gospel truth alighted on my soul from Jeremiah 31:3 where God says: "yes, I have loved you with an everlasting love, and with my lovingkindness (grace) have I drawn you." The verse completely blew me away. First, I saw that *eternal* did not just mean "endless time" or "forever in time," but also "outside of time." God is eternal not because He lives forever, but because he dwells outside time, before time was created. Then I saw that, in Christ, God's love for me was not just forever; it was outside time. In other words, before time began and after time ends, God will always love me!

If this is true, what then could I do to diminish or even increase His love for me? **NOTHING!** That is the truth of the gospel! What a powerful word! *Nothing!*

So we see why Paul says in Galatians 2 that he refused to yield or submit to these Jewish Christians who came to pervert the gospel message, not even for a moment. He did so in order that "the truth of the gospel" may continue in the lives of those who had believed. The fact is, rules and regulations and laws of people or God cannot change weak humans held under the bondage and power of sin or ourselves. No! Only the truth of the gospel has the power to save. But when that gospel message is mixed up and perverted with a "false gospel" of Jesus plus something—we eliminate the ability of the gospel to save.

Let me conclude this chapter by focusing on the one truth of the gospel that Paul mentions in our text. He says because of the gospel - if indeed it is true that God has done *everything* that needs to be done for us to be saved - then we are *free* from any obligations of the law. We have liberty. In other words, we have freedom. And our acute sense and experience of it is the most powerful evidence that we know and truly believe the truth of the gospel. What you do with that freedom is very important; we will come to that shortly. But if, after you finish listening to a message, or you become involved with someone or with a group and your sense of freedom is diminished, *run!* As Paul would say later in Galatians 5:1: "it was for freedom that Christ set you free. Stand fast in that freedom."

Paul continued by showing at least three ways the gospel

makes us free. First, knowing the truth of the gospel made Paul free from the guilt and penalty of his sinful life (Galatians 1:13–16). Paul says that one thing the gospel made him realize was that, in Jesus, before the foundation of the world, before Paul ever did one good thing or one bad thing, God had chosen him and called him. On the day Paul received salvation, all the momentous events that took place on that Damascus road, and the preaching (announcement) of Ananias, came together to reveal to Paul what God had done for Paul *before Paul was even born*. And on that day, Paul *finally* believed it. And because he believed, he owned what God had done, and it freed him from the pain and guilt of his murderous, sinful life. Consequently, he was then able to go about boldly preaching the same gospel he once tried to destroy. Do you have freedom to boldly preach the gospel, regardless of the life you may have lived in the past or even the life you are living now? Do you realize that in Jesus, you are chosen before the foundation of the world to be holy and without blame in God's sight? In humanity's sight, you may be blamable, you may not talk to God, you may not have the qualifications, you may even have committed many fatal sins and have many fatal flaws. But if you are in Christ (and you are), then you have been chosen and declared *holy* (separated unto God) *before* anything was ever made or ever happened. Can you imagine how dramatically different your life would be and how much freedom you could experience if you simply looked past all your present situation to believe this truth? Your life will be emancipated, and a mighty boldness to declare God's word with power will manifest in your life.

Secondly, knowing the truth of the gospel made Paul free from seeking to please people (Galatians 1:10). Knowing the truth of the gospel, that because of what Jesus did, God now loves and accepts you, no matter what, cures your deepest insecurities. The truth is that in Jesus, in spite of all your defects, God accepts you 100 percent. There's nothing more to do to increase God's love or acceptance of you. There's *nothing* you could do to decrease God's love for you. Therefore, you owe no one anything but love. No person can or should make you do anything. You do not need to persuade anyone that you are anointed, spiritual, holy, or accepted. No! In Jesus, you have been accepted and perfected forever! Finally, knowing the truth of the gospel made Paul free to do things purely out of love for the God who saved him. It made it possible for Paul to voluntarily choose to be a bondservant of Jesus (Galatians 1:10) and to eagerly serve the poor (2:10). People often ask: "But if I have now been accepted by God and perfected because of what Jesus did rather than because of what I do, then why should I make an effort to live a godly life?" The answer is this: you *should* make an effort out of love for what God has done for you and out of your love for God. This love is now your new nature, the nature of your Father God, the nature of love. The only reason your Father in heaven does anything is love, because God is love. Paul says to do all things out of love (1 Corinthians 16:14). Anything not done 100

> **Do everything in love - 1 Corinthians 16:14 (NIV)**

percent out of love is nothing (1 Corinthians 13:1-4).

I usually ask a question to try to make this point clearer. Is helping an old woman across the street a good thing? Most people will answer yes, it is. But if you think about it carefully, you'd concede that "it depends" is the correct answer. If I helped the old woman across the street so that I could then turn around and say: "God, because I have helped this woman, you should do X for me." Whom did I really help—the old woman or me? It was me. But if I know that God has done all for me in Jesus with no contribution from me, this truth of the gospel enables me to see an old woman and still decide to help her, not to earn anything from God (because God has blessed me with everything already) but out of love for God and the woman. I help the woman because of love. That's who I am. It's a good thing to do, and it is good to do a good thing. It is my nature, just like my Father's. Brothers and sisters, only the truth of the gospel can produce this response in the lives of humans. This false gospel that teaches us to earn our acceptance with God destroys love in our hearts, and it is this absence of love that made this false gospel so dangerous. It strikes at the very heart of what God wants to produce in His children - love as the only motive for all our actions.

Love upends a lot of what many of us have been taught about godly living. We have traditionally been taught, "do good, get good; do bad, get bad." We are told to avoid sin, or we lose our salvation. We will miss heaven, miss the rapture, end up in hell, or face some severe punishment from God. This approach is inherently selfish, and selfishness is a sin. It is selfish because of the reason why you are asked to do good. It is for your own personal benefit. Suppose someone says, "I forgive her because I do not want to be in unforgiveness when the rapture happens, and I don't want to miss it." That person is acting out of an ungodly, selfish motive. That motive is **NOT** godly; our Father God does not forgive someone because "if he does not, he will be evicted from heaven!" God forgives because He loves; He forgives because forgiving is inherently good. And doing good is good. God's nature is love and goodness.

Can you now see why the gospel of God's grace is so crucial? The gospel of God's grace is the good news that the finished work of Jesus plus *nothing* we do is the foundation of our acceptance with God. Without this truth of the gospel, it is impossible for a Christian to be genuinely unselfish in any act of goodness. It is the absence of this gospel of God's grace that makes "all our righteousnesses to be filthy rags" (Isaiah 64:6) because, without it, every single act of righteousness we do is rooted in selfishness. But when we know that nothing we do or don't do has *any impact* on whether God loves us or accepts us; when we know that the *only basis* of God's acceptance of us is the finished work of Jesus - we can now choose to do good works simply out of love, and simply because it is our nature to be good and to love. Now we can forgive, not because if we do not forgive, we will miss heaven (we won't), but because we love so much, we would never hold a grudge. We forgive to free the other person because we want to demonstrate our love to them. We know that the guilt they are feeling over how they treated us locks them up in a prison, and we want to release them from that prison because we love them. We help people because doing good deeds for others is who we are. Being good is our nature.

I once heard Dr. Tim Keller, pastor of New York's Redeemer Presbyterian Church, bring this point out so powerfully with a short parable in one of his audio messages. He asked listeners to imagine a young man who, from when he was a boy of ten, went to his great-aunt's house every day to help her out. He would be there from eight in the morning until six in the evening. He would keep her company, run errands for her, and help her around the house. He skipped playing soccer with his friends to help his great-aunt. He missed out on dates with his girlfriend. He essentially denied himself all the pleasures of youth in order to meet his great-aunt's needs. Then one day, when he was about twenty-two years old, as he was wrapping up his work for the day and getting ready to leave for home, his great-aunt took him aside and told him that earlier that day she had spoken to her attorney to permanently and irrevocably will *all* her estate to him. She made the transfer permanent and irrevocable, such that not even she could revoke it later because she did not want anyone to come later to convince her to change her mind. The preacher then said: what this young man does at eight the next morning will reveal for the first time the true motive of his heart. If he does not show up as usual, then we know that all along, he never really loved his great-aunt. Can you imagine that? Despite all of his visible, helpful actions, he was being selfish and just doing it for himself. What an evil person, right? Aha, but we only got to know that now because of grace - the unmerited, unconditional, permanent, and irrevocable act of his great-aunt. But,

The Truth of the Gospel

and oh, how beautiful it would be, if this young man, after having been told this, still shows up at eight in the morning, still denies himself, and still serves his great-aunt as usual. Then we'd know for sure that *love and love alone* is and has always been his motive. Again, what revealed this? **Grace** revealed it, the unmerited, unconditional, permanent, and irrevocable act of his great-aunt.

So we see that the truth of the gospel does not only reveal to us the truth about who God is and what God has done for us. It also reveals to us the truth about who we truly are. One of the problems the law caused was a situation where people served God outwardly with their mouths and outward behavior, but in their hearts, they were far from God. God talked about this in Isaiah 29:13: *"Therefore the Lord said: "Since these people draw near with their mouths And honor Me with their lips, But have removed their hearts far from Me, And their fear toward Me is taught by the commandment of men.* In this verse, the Lord is saying that when people worship God by keeping commandments, it is impossible to know if they are truly serving him from their hearts. In most cases, they are not serving him from their hearts. They are keeping the commandment because people expect them, for whatever reason, so to do. The gospel of God's grace, by removing the requirement to keep commandments in order to be commended to God, exposes for the first time what is really in your heart and what kind of person you are. I remember a lady who once gave testimony of how the Lord convinced her to quit wearing jewelry and using cosmetics. However, the testimony was robbed of its power when we later discovered that she belonged to a denomination that insisted that members had to quit using jewelry to be promoted to certain leadership levels. You can see how it is now impossible to confirm whether her actions were truly borne out of the Lord speaking to her, or whether she took those steps in order to serve in her denomination. We will never know if, indeed, this was her heart yielding to God or if this was an action to please the leadership of her denomination until she is in an environment where using those things does not matter. Then she will be who she really is.

This is what makes the truth of the gospel of grace so powerful. When people are truly free to do whatever they will, they will be who they truly are. But if they are in an environment of law and legalism, people will pretend or modify their behavior, but their hearts will remain unchanged and unconverted. And the moment you put them in a different environment, you see their true natures manifest. Jesus said: "by their fruits, you will know them. A good tree will produce good fruits; an evil tree produces evil fruits" (See Matthew 7:17-19). We must also remember that He taught this in the context of the new kingdom he was ushering in, the kingdom of the reign of God's grace where people can be truly free to behave as they actually are. The tree Jesus was describing was a complete living thing; it wasn't rigged by science to produce externally what it's not internally. Let a tree be truly free to be what it is, and it will produce its fruit. This is what the gospel does, it reveals to people who they really are. The scriptures say to readers that either "all things are lawful" or "you are free to do whatever you want, but it does not change how God relates to you." Having said that, God then watches to see exactly what you will do to discern whether you are an evil tree or a good tree.

I beseech you, therefore, to do all you can to vehemently resist linking your acceptance by God or of yourself to anything you do or don't do. Similarly, resist any efforts from people, pastors, prophets, Christians, or non-Christians who make the same requirements. Consider Paul, who vehemently resisted that Titus be circumcised. When you carefully read this account, you will see that Paul has no issue with circumcision. Years later, Paul wanted to increase his chances of reaching a Jewish audience. He encouraged Timothy, his half-Gentile, half-Jewish companion, to be circumcised (Acts 16:3) so that those whom Timothy was going to preach to could well receive him. Later on, we see that Paul himself shaved his hair to participate in a Jewish ceremony. So Paul had no problem with Jewish rituals and traditions. What he had a problem with was for Titus, or anyone who believes in Jesus for their salvation, to be "compelled" to do anything else to be assured of their salvation. Having been saved, our goal must be to reject the devil's lies by pursuing, discovering, and embracing the truth of the gospel. That truth has the power to produce the result of our salvation in our lives. We must reject every attempt to make us do anything, even if it is just one thing, in addition to believing in Jesus to be saved. It is an attempt to steal our freedom. We must vehemently reject these efforts and give them no place in our lives, not even for a second. If we do, if we give in even on that one thing, we start sliding down a slippery slope that will find us eventually living in guilt, living to please people, and operating out of duty rather than love for God. As we can see, this approach robs us of all the wonderful blessings in the truth of the gospel.

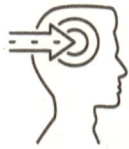

DEEPENING YOUR UNDERSTANDING

- What do you understand as the truth or truths of the gospel? Give examples of some we tend to forget.

- In what ways do church members become people-pleasers in their specific denominations? How could this affect someone's practice of Christianity?

- What is the difference between Titus being circumcised and Timothy being circumcised? Can this translate to other works of the law?

APPLYING WHAT YOU HAVE LEARNED

- What steps can you take today to preserve your liberty and freedom in Christ as a Christian?

- Why do you think this message of freedom in Christ is not preached more? How could you present the message so that it is not abused, but understood?

- Make a list of gospel truths that you know. How could living your life according to these truths change you? What can you do to make this happen?

CHAPTER 4

Obeying the Truth of the Gospel

But when I saw that they walked not uprightly <u>according to the truth of the gospel</u>, I said unto Peter before them all, If thou, being a Jew, livest after the manner of Gentiles, and not as do the Jews, why compellest thou the Gentiles to live as do the Jews? I am crucified with Christ: nevertheless, I live; yet not I, but Christ liveth in me: and the life which I now live in the flesh I live by the faith of the Son of God, who loved me and gave himself for me. I do not frustrate the grace of God: for if righteousness come by the law, then Christ is dead in vain (Galatians 2:14, 20–21 KJVS).

I recently discovered a phrase in the New Testament that I am not sure many Christians have reflected on. It is the phrase "obeying the truth," "obedience to the truth," or "obeying the gospel." You see it used in Romans 2:8, Galatians 3:1, and 1 Peter 1:22, among others. This is a curious phrase. You obey commands and believe or acknowledge truths. How on earth can one obey the truth? For example, how can one obey the truth that the "sun is 92.96 million miles away from the earth"? It must mean more than just acknowledging that fact. To "obey that truth" would mean living your life in recognition of that truth. Even though you may not see, smell, taste, hear, or feel it, you know and believe that the Sun is in the sky, and so you order your life accordingly. This is how the gospel of God's grace produces a life of holiness and righteousness. You are not motivated by the fear of missing out because of breaking laws. Instead, you have a positive motivation to manifest and to produce all that is true about you in Christ Jesus.

Renowned contemporary Christian preacher Andrew Wommack would say that the difference between the Bible's Old Testament and the New Testament is more than just the blank page in between. In the Old Testament, under the law, the Jews were required to obey God's commands. According to the old covenant entered into between God and the Israelites at Mount Sinai, this was the basis of being accepted by God. How people could ever agree to obey to the letter every single command God gave as the basis of being accepted by God, I would never know. But God knew humans and the human heart; they could never be faithful no matter how hard they tried. The human heart is full of sin and deceit. And so God announced through His prophets a new covenant, one where God's acceptance would not be based on what *we do*, but on what

> It is a mistake to attempt to correct people by just pointing them to what God commands them to do – to the laws of the Bible. Rather, they should be invited to respond in love to what God has done for them – to the truths of the gospel.

Obeying the Truth of the Gospel

God does to us, in us, and for us. In this new covenant, God will radically and completely change us from the inside out. Going forward, the lives we live will not be motivated by the outward keeping of God's laws. Instead, our lives will be reflections and evidence that God has *already transformed us and accepts us* on the basis of what God has already done in us. In the New Covenant, we do not obey commands; we obey this truth of what God has done. We live as if what God has done in us is true, because it is. It is, therefore, a fundamental mistake when New Testament believers attempt to correct bad behavior or motivate good behavior by pointing people to commands and laws in the Bible, especially from the Old Testament! They should rather be pointing people to the truth of what God has done and rousing each other to walk according to these truths.

In the congregation I attend, every once in a while, we hold question-and-answer sessions. These sessions allow our attendees to ask any question related to the Christian faith. I remember one of those sessions when a young adult asked, "Is it okay to listen to worldly music?" In most Christian gatherings, when such a question is posed, we often want to go to the Bible, find a Bible verse that goes something like "thou shalt not..." or "thou shalt..." and then say: "hear, hear, this is what the Bible says; go ye and do or do not do likewise." The problem is, while this is one of the most

> The Bible is not primarily a book of rules and regulations but a book of revelation.

popular uses of the Bible, it is *NOT* the reason why we have the Bible. The Bible is not primarily a book of rules and regulations; it is primarily a book of *revelation*. The Bible is the revelation of God and humanity to us. The Bible reveals to us who God our Father is, His heart of love toward us, and all He has done to bring us, his errant, rebellious children, back home. Even the rules and regulations in the Bible are included to help us see this point.

When Paul confronted Peter in the verses we are considering, he did not, as we often do, quote a commandment in the law (Bible). Paul could have easily gone to Peter, quoted the passage where Jesus called the Pharisees and Sadducees hypocrites, and said: "Peter, Jesus said that what you have just done is hypocrisy. Repent or perish! Turn or burn!" The problem would be, however, that Peter would have quoted back to Paul from Paul's writing that "if anyone is a fornicator and an adulterer do not mingle with such a person, no not even to eat with them…" and then go ahead to point out how he caught some of those pagans in sexual immorality the night before. Then Paul would have countered with Peter's writing that Jesus set an example for us; if Jesus ate and drank with sinners, Peter should have done so also. Both of them would have ended up finding Bible passages excusing or accusing each other's actions, with each person defending himself and his position.

And this is what we see happening among many of us Christians today. We have resorted to using the Bible as a book of rules and regulations to modify behavior and motivate good actions. Everyone is justifying or excusing himself or herself using the Bible. At the same time, we accuse and attack one another using the same Bible we have just used to excuse ourselves! I have been a Christian long enough to realize that if I used the Bible in this way, I could justify any of my actions or condemn anyone's action. But Paul addressed this issue with Peter in the light of the truth of the gospel. An overview of the situation would be helpful in appreciating the power of how Paul handled the situation.

Recall that Antioch was the church that sent Paul and Barnabas off to take the good news about what God did for humanity through Jesus to the Gentile nations. While most of the people there were either Jewish proselytes or devout Gentiles who had converted to Christianity, a good number of them were non-Jewish or Gentile converts. Paul and Barnabas had been instrumental in strengthening this church. Apparently, Peter had come to visit Paul and Barnabas in Antioch. Before certain leaders came down from Jerusalem to visit, Peter had no problem fellowshipping and eating with the Gentile Christians. However, it appeared that when these men that James sent arrived, Peter felt condemned and blamed. The Greek word *Kataginosko*, which Paul used in Galatians 2:11 and is translated "blame" (KJV) or "condemned" (NASB/NIV) and is used only three times in the New Testament. The other two times it is used is in 1 John 3:20–21:

"For if our heart condemns us, God is greater than our heart and knows all things. Beloved, if our heart does not condemn us, we have confidence toward God."

It is important to note that the word here is different from the regular word for *condemn* in the New Testament, *katakri-*

no. *Katakrino* means to be judged worthy of punishment as a result of having broken some law. *Kataginosko* means to be accused of wrongdoing, to be put on trial, or to be blamed. In order words, to be indicted, accused but not yet judged, and condemned. Reading in context, it appears that these Jewish Christians that James sent when they arrived in Antioch and found Peter eating with the Gentile Christians, they accused him, or blamed him or put him under indictment, but that was not the real problem. The real issue was that Peter allowed himself to be so blamed and indicted that he withdrew and stopped eating with the Gentile Christians.

I want you to transport yourself into that scenario and picture what is happening here. What accusation or blame was leveled against Peter? Did someone say to him that he had broken one of the Jewish laws that prohibited eating with non-Jews? Or did they point out to Peter that the food the Gentiles prepared was not kosher—i.e., it did not meet the Jewish dietary laws? Perhaps pork, shrimp, or crab was served? Or perhaps, what they blamed Peter for or accused him of was that the food was purchased in Gentile markets, and everyone knew the Gentile butchers and farmers always sacrificed their produce to their idols before bringing it to the market to sell.

Whatever it was, the accusation was leveled at Peter. He accepted it and consequently attempted to remedy the situation by withdrawing from the Gentile brethren and eating with them. I am so glad Paul did not say that Peter was *katakrino*— judged and condemned by God. Alleluia! For according to Romans 8:1—"there is therefore now no condemnation—no *katakrino*—to them who are in Christ Jesus.

This is the truth of the gospel. However, it is possible to experience *Kataginosko*—blame, accusations, fault finding, and a sense of guilt in your heart. As a result, you are deprived of the blessings God has for you in Jesus.

We see this happen quite a bit today among believers. Christians find fault, blame and indict other Christians whom God has not accused, blamed, or condemned. We blame them for how they present the gospel message, for the cars they drive, and the houses they live in. We blame them for the clothes they wear. We blame them for how they style their hair. We look for fault and blame others, forgetting that because in Christ we are not justified by anything we do or not do, we cannot therefore be condemned by anything we do or not do. What could not save us cannot damn us or unsave us. Many times, as John pointed out in 1 John 3, it is we who allow our own hearts to blame us and condemn us—when God does not condemn us— because, in Christ Jesus, we cannot be condemned.

Whatever the reason that Peter allowed himself to be so filled with blame and condemnation, Paul was having none of this! Paul said when he saw that they were not "acting in line with the truth of the gospel," he confronted Peter. It is important that you pause and think about this. Paul is saying here that "if you believe the truth of the gospel, if it is indeed true that God has done what we preach as the good news of what God has done for us in Christ, then there is no way you would think it is okay for you to live in this way." In other words, there is a way of living that is "in line with" and "according to" the truth of the gospel, i.e., it acknowledges the truth of the gospel as true. There is also a way of living that is not in line with and not according to the truth of the gospel, i.e., it does not acknowledge the truth of the gospel as true. In other words, if the truth of the gospel is indeed true, then you cannot be acting in this way. But if you believe that the way you are acting is okay, then by your actions, you are saying that the truth of the gospel is not true. You cannot have it both ways. It is either one or the other. Let's drill down on this point in this specific case.

What Paul essentially did was to remind Peter and his fellow Jewish Christians, including his companion Barnabas who was led astray by this hypocrisy, one of the truths of the gospel. The truth he reminded them was the fact that God had accepted all people, including Peter, in Christ, without their compliance to and with the laws of Moses. In other words, God did not accept Jews such as Peter, Paul, and the Jewish believers — who were not "sinful Gentiles" — because of the laws they kept, but because of Jesus's sacrifice. In spite of how well or poorly they kept the law, God set the law aside as a requirement for acceptance into God's family for all who are in Jesus. Because of His love for them, He accepted them in Jesus. Paul then said, "If this is true, how could someone accuse you of sinning and being condemned by God by referring to the same law that God put aside when He accepted you in Jesus?" Both of these points could not be true at the same time! In other words, God cannot accept you without the law and then turn around and judge you a sinner by the same law he set aside when he accepted you!

Furthermore, Paul went on, if it is indeed true that God accepted you without the law, why then would He reject the Gentiles because they are not keeping the law? Both of these points could not be true at the same time! If God accepted you without the keeping of the law, he could not turn around and insist that Gentiles must embrace the law in order for Him to accept them! Finally, if indeed God accepts you without your compliance with the law, why then do you reject Gentile Christians because they are not compliant with the law? Again, both of these cannot be true at the same time! You cannot say that God accepts you *without* the law, but you will only accept your Gentile brothers and sisters if they keep the law! In other words, if God has done it for you, why would you not "obey that truth"—live as if that truth is also true for your Gentile brothers and sisters? If the gospel is true, Paul says to Peter, then "obey the truth"—live as if it is true (1 Peter 1:22). Alleluia! What a powerful confrontation!

There is a huge difference between living by the gospel and living by the law. Take your time and read the last two paragraphs again and notice the key difference between how to confront with the gospel versus confronting with the law. This is how the gospel can do what the law could *never* do. The law says, "I do this so that God will do that." Conversely, the gospel says: "Because God has done this, therefore, I do that." It is *rooted* in faith in what God did. The gospel is a response to what you believe that God has already done. For example, Paul says, "I am eager to care for the poor and needy. Why? Not just because the Bible commands it, but because the gospel truth is that I was once poor, wretched, spiritually needy, morally bankrupt, and totally unable to care for myself. Yet Jesus, who was rich, gave up all his wealth for me that I, through his poverty, may be rich" (2 Corinthians 8:9). If that is true, and if that happened to me, how then can I see poor or needy people around me and not do for them what was done for me? That would not be living according to the truth of the gospel. Both of these situations cannot be true - I could not be a poor and needy individual whom God helped and not make myself available for God to help other poor and needy persons through me. If I do not help someone who is poor and needy, it only evinces that in my heart of hearts, I never truly believed the truth that I was deeply poor and needy before God helped me.

If the truth of the gospel is that all my sins have been paid for and forgiven in Jesus — *all* of them — what, then, do I do when I sin? I do not grovel in guilt, fear, and self-pity, No! I obey the truth — I come boldly to the throne of grace, where two thousand years ago, before I was born, Jesus paid the price for the forgiveness of *all* my sins — to *receive* the forgiveness and mercy *already* provided for me! That is *obeying* the truth. In the same way, because God has forgiven *all* my sins, I should also forgive others their sins against me. It **cannot** be true that God has forgiven *all* my sins in Jesus on the cross two thousand years ago but did not forgive the sin of my sister or brother in Christ who sinned against me. When I refuse to forgive my sister or brother, I am holding against her something even God has not held against her. That would be making me equal to or greater than God, as Joseph said in Genesis 50:19-20. This is why unforgiveness is the number one proof that someone has never really accepted the sacrifice of Jesus as the basis of their salvation.

If it is true that in Christ Jesus, he who was rich became poor that I may be rich, then I am rich. If it is indeed true, that in Jesus, God has given me all things that pertain to life and godliness; that all spiritual blessings in the heavenly realm have been given to me; and if it is indeed true that *all things* are mine — then how can I not be a generous person? Generosity is the natural outflow in the lives of people who believe in the truth of the gospel and have decided to "obey that truth" — or live as if it is true. And so, as a result, I am generous. I give out of the little that I may seem to have, knowing that I have been truly blessed by God more than I can see. Regardless of physical circumstances or situations in the natural world, I accept that the gospel is true and live by it.

Many New Testament phrases make this point and, once we have this understanding of "obeying the truth", they may begin to hold powerful new meanings for us. Examples of these phrases include:

- *Freely you have received; freely give (Matthew 10:8).*
- *Love one another, as I have loved you (John 13:34).*
- *We love because He first loved us (1 John 4:7–19).*
- *Forgive one another as God has forgiven you in Christ (Ephesians 4:32).*

In all of these examples, you can see that we are instructed to "act" because of what has been done to us rather than "act" so that something will be done for us. We see then from Paul's confrontation with Peter that it is not really how we see people that determines how we relate with others. It is how we see *ourselves* that determines how we relate with others. In other words, unless you believe as true what God has said about you in the gospel and live in accordance with that truth, i.e., obey the truth, you will not be able to live correctly. Peter lapsed in obedience to the truth, and Paul corrected him—not by throwing a commandment at him but by reminding him of the truth of the gospel. *Therefore, to live correctly, we must focus on pointing people to the truth of the gospel*, not to laws and rules! We must go to Mt. Calvary, not to Mt. Sinai. Let's not frustrate the grace of God. You will not persuade people to live correctly by giving them laws and rules. Israel in the Old Testament repeatedly proved that righteousness would never come by futile attempts to keep the law. Inspire people to live correctly by showing them the truth of the gospel. God, through Christ, now lives in them. And through how they relate with others, God can now be a blessing to others just as He has been a blessing to them.

So, when we encountered that question about worldly music in our church bible study, I answered by asking a question: "Why do you want to—or have to—listen to worldly music?" You may be listening to it as part of your job, such as a radio station or media house. If that is the case, you had better be a very good listener of worldly music so you can do your job well. But if you are listening because you are looking to worldly music to get something that, according to the truth of the gospel, God has already provided for you in Jesus, then you have a problem. It may not be just worldly music. It may be sex, food, gospel music, church, your family, your spouse, your job, your business, your career, and several other things in this world. If we're not careful, these things could take the place of Jesus in our lives as Lord and Savior. This was why Paul said, "although all things are lawful to me—i.e., in Jesus, nothing I do can condemn me—yet I will not allow anything to take God's place in my life." The bottom line is this: if the gospel is true, then live as though it is.

DEEPENING YOUR UNDERSTANDING

What does this all mean?

- Living according to the truth of the gospel is sometimes called "living from the inside out." Living according to the law is sometimes called "living from the outside in." Why is one doomed to fail and the other the only means for righteous living?

- If someone is not living according to the truth, it means he or she is living according to a lie. What are the common lies Christians believe about themselves that often lead to bondage, satanic oppression, or defeated lives?

- "What God is to you, He will be through you to others." How does this truth explain the common accusation that Christians tend to be very judgmental people? How could this truth be the key to becoming more loving and accepting of people?

- How is Paul's rebuke of Peter similar to how Paul responded in Romans 6 to the question "shall we continue in sin that grace may abound?" or of his correction of the immorality of the Corinthian church in 1 Corinthians 6?

- Discuss: The way we treat others is not a reflection of how we see them. Rather, it is a reflection of how we see ourselves. Why? Why not?

APPLYING WHAT YOU HAVE LEARNED

Now, what do I do?

- What areas do you struggle with in your life? Ask the Holy Spirit: *"What lie(s) do I believe about God, about myself, and about sin that are at the root of these struggles?"* Pause and listen to Him speak to you. Renounce those things as lies in Jesus's name.

- Ask the Holy Spirit: *"Lord, what truth must I believe and start obeying so that I can experience victory in these areas?"* Pause and listen to Him speak to you. Then receive and confess those truths in Jesus's name.

- Think about someone you know who is not living correctly. How would you admonish this person as Paul did with Peter—not by finding a rule or command in the Bible, but instead reminding them of the truth of the gospel?

CHAPTER 5

Living in the Flesh versus Living in the Spirit

O foolish Galatians! Who has bewitched you that you should not obey the truth, before whose eyes Jesus Christ was portrayed among you as crucified? This only I want to learn from you: Did you receive the Spirit by the works of the law, or by the hearing of faith? – Are you so foolish? Having begun in the Spirit, are you now being made perfect by the flesh? Have you suffered so many things in vain – if indeed it was in vain? Therefore He who supplies the Spirit to you and works miracles among you, does He do it by the works of the law, or by the hearing of faith? (Galatians 3:1 – 5 NKJV).

An important but often misunderstood concept in the New Testament is "living or walking in the flesh," together with its corollary: "living or walking in Spirit." Until recently, I had the same understanding most Christians today have of what Paul meant when he used the word "the flesh" (Greek: sarx). I used to understand the flesh as that part of my nature that was bad, ugly, and anti-God. The flesh was everything in my natural, normal being that produced bad actions, poor choices, evil desires, jealous or envious feelings, and tragic outcomes. From the flesh came everything opposed to wise and joyful living. The flesh produced sexual immoralities, lusts, and desires that were contrary to my desires to serve God. It caused me to lust; it caused me to be lazy and and go weeks or months without meaningful communication with God. "The flesh" was responsible for my finding it hard to forgive, even though I knew this was something I ought to do!

And so I was taught and came to believe that "my flesh" needed to be subdued, mortified, crucified, pummeled, subjugated, tortured, and forced to obey the word of God, or else it would doom me. At the same time, I was not exactly sure how to define this "flesh." Was it my mind, my soul, or my human body? I was not sure if the flesh had been crucified with Christ or if I was to crucify my flesh. Or was it my mind that needed to be transformed rather than mortified and neglected? When I looked at my Christian life, one thing was clear: I struggled with sins and negative behaviors that I was told came from my flesh. What was not clear was how exactly I was supposed to beat this thing. In this chapter, I would like to share one way of understanding "the flesh" and how that understanding, together with what we have learned about the truth of the gospel, could help us increasingly gain victory in the areas where we struggle to live a Godly life.

A common and useful guideline in biblical hermeneutics (the science of interpreting the Bible) is a principle known as the "law of the first mention." This law states that to understand a particular word or doctrine, it is often very helpful to find the first place in Scripture where that word or doctrine is revealed and study that passage. The thinking is that the place where a concept is first mentioned in the Bible would most likely give the simplest and clearest presentation of the concept; subsequent mentions now seeking to develop on that initial foundation that has been laid. This, by the way, is the reason why the book of Genesis, where so many concepts and words are mentioned for the first time, holds the key to unlocking so many truths of the gospel explained further in other books of the Bible. Now, if we remember that Galatians was the first book written by the Apostle Paul, a lot of the confusion centering on the concepts of "living in the flesh" versus "living in the Spirit" would be sorted out. I will cover the basics of these concepts in this chapter. In a later chapter, I will dive into the practical aspects.

Those of us in Charismatic/Pentecostal circles live for and long for the days of revival—the days when many souls shall turn to Jesus through a mighty outpouring of the Holy Spirit, with signs and wonders following. In the verses that opened this chapter, Paul gives some insight into how we, like the Galatian Gentile Christians, experience a mighty manifestation of the power of God when the gospel of what God has done for us through Jesus is preached. He also touched on how we could short-circuit God's power in our lives as Christians and thus delay the revival we seek. In Galatians 3:2 and 5, Paul suggests that the receiving of the Holy Spirit, the ministration of the baptism of the Holy Spirit, and the working of miracles among the Galatians did not happen because of the "works of the law" but because of the "hearing of faith." He then proceeds to call out the Galatians, calling them fools for having begun "in the Spirit" but now trying to attain maturity "in the flesh."

Now, given the way the books of the New Testament are

arranged in our Bibles today, it is easy for someone to fail to realize that these verses were the first mention of the words "in the Spirit" and "in the flesh" by Paul in the New Testament. Paul ended up writing at least thirteen books of the New Testament, including the book of Romans, where he would extensively use the phrases "in the flesh" and "in the Spirit." But Galatians 3 is the first place and his first mention of these phrases, which means, following the principle of the first mention, carefully studying this passage and understanding what Paul meant when he wrote these words to the Galatian Christians, we ought to gain a solid foundation and understanding of what Paul means when he uses the phrases "in the flesh" and "in the Spirit" in his other thirteen books.

> To live by grace is the same thing as to walk in the Spirit. It is to affirm that what God has done for you through Jesus in the Spirit is the ONLY reason why God accepts you and continues to accept you.

So Galatians 3, we see Paul contrasting for the Galatian Christians two concepts that result from which version of the gospel they accepted. On the one hand, there is a way of living your life according to the gospel that says faith alone in what God has done for you through Jesus is the ONLY reason why God accepts and continues to accept you. He calls this the "hearing of faith" because it has nothing to do with what you do, or do not, do. You only receive it by believing that it is true. On the other hand, there is a way of living your

Living in the Flesh versus Living in the Spirit

life according to the "other" gospel, the one that says it is your faith in what God has done for you through Jesus PLUS your efforts to please God that are the reasons why God accepts or continues to accept you. He calls this "the works of the law" because these efforts are derived from the laws given by God, found in the Old Testament and the Bible. In the Law, you find the list of "good" things to do and "bad" things to avoid. Paul reminds the Galatians that when they got saved by believing the gospel of what God had done for them, they had begun their Christian walk "in the Spirit." However, by listening to the Jewish Christians who were attempting to get them to revert to the works of the law in order to be saved or continue to be saved, Paul says they were now trying to achieve maturity or perfection "in the flesh" or "the works of the law." Paul then asks if they received the baptism of the Holy Spirit and miracles by the "hearing of faith" or by the "works of the law."

Please pause here and read those verses again until you can see the contrasts Paul lays out. If you do, what you would observe is that in these verses where Paul for the very first time introduced the concepts of "in the spirit" and "in the flesh," Paul associates the "hearing of faith" with "living or walking in the Spirit," and "the works of the law" with "living in the flesh." Put another way, to "live in the Spirit" simply means to conduct your life believing that what God said He did for you in Jesus is true. This is what we have also earlier called "obeying the truth" or "living according to the truth of the gospel." In other words, to "live in the Spirit" is really not some mystical, exotic, and mysterious way of living, doable by the most "spiritual" of us. Anyone who comes to know some truth about themselves in Jesus contained in the gospel and begins to make an effort to live it out or live as if that truth is indeed true - even though outwardly there does not seem to be any signs that it is - that person is "walking in the Spirit!"

At the same time, to "live in the flesh" means to conduct your life as if what you observe in the natural world, what you see, smell, hear, taste, and feel, is true. More specifically, if your view of your relationship with God is based on your observation with your natural senses of how well you are keeping the laws of God, you are walking in the flesh, even if you are doing a darn good job observing those laws! It is as simple as that.

Paul is saying if you want to live in the Spirit, ignore what you observe in the natural and live as if what God has done for you in Jesus is true. And this includes that you are accepted and declared righteous by God — not by what you do or not do, but because of what Jesus did. On the other hand, if you ignore what God has done for you in Jesus and live as if what you observe in the natural world — what you see, taste, smell, hear, and feel — is what is true, you are living in the flesh. This includes living as if God accepts you, blesses you, and listens to your prayers based on what you do or do not do and how well you are keeping God's laws — all of which are things we can easily observe.

This is extremely powerful — especially if you use this as the background to read other passages of the Bible, such as Galatians 5 and Romans 8, where Paul would go on to talk extensively about "living in the flesh" and "living in the spirit." Paul is using these phrases to describe a way of living, a mindset, a philosophy of life. He is not speaking of some mystical nature or thing that dwells in you and is causing you to behave in a certain way. "Living in the flesh" or "living in the Spirit" is a description of your fundamental mindset, a philosophy, or a way of conducting your life. It is a way of describing human choice — how you have chosen to live, a choice that will lead to specific, predictable outcomes. Let's use this simple definition in some very famous verses and see how profound this is.

In Romans 8:1, we read: *"There is therefore now no condemnation to those who are in Christ Jesus, who do not walk according to the flesh, but according to the Spirit"* (NKJV). Most modern translations do not include the last phrase, "...who do not walk according to the flesh, but according to the Spirit," rightly showing that this phrase is not found in the most ancient manuscripts. However, understanding what Paul means by walking according to the flesh and walking according to the Spirit, as we saw in Galatians 3, the phrase does not subtract from the meaning of the verse but enhances it. If you took the definitions of "living in the flesh" and "living in the Spirit" that we read from Paul in Galatians 3 and substituted them in this verse, Romans 8:1 then reads as follows:

> *There is therefore now no condemnation to those who are in Christ Jesus, who do not live by what they observe in the natural such as how well they are keeping the works of the law, but live according to the truth of what God has done for them in Jesus, including the fact that they are forever accepted by God in Jesus!*

In Romans 8:1, Paul is therefore saying that you will lose all your sense of guilt and condemnation the moment you quit measuring yourself by how well you keep the law and begin to view yourself from the perspective of what God has done for you in Jesus. Praise God! This is consistent with the point he makes throughout the book of Romans.

Let's look at a couple more examples to drive the point home. Take a look at Romans 8:5-8: *"For those who live according to the flesh set their minds on the things of the flesh, but those who live according to the Spirit, the things of the Spirit. For to be carnally minded is death, but to be spiritually minded is life and peace. Because the carnal mind is enmity against God; for it is not subject to the law of God, nor indeed can be. So then, those who are in the flesh cannot please God."* (NKJV). Again replacing "living in the flesh" with "living as if what you observe in the natural, such as how well you keep the works of the law" and "living in the Spirit" with "living as if what God has done for you in Jesus is true" these verses jump out with powerful clarity: *For those [who live as if what they observe in the natural is true, such as how well they keep the works of the law], set their minds on the things [they observe in the natural] but those who [live as if what God has done for them in Jesus is true], set their mind on the things [God has done for them in Jesus]. For to [live by focusing your mind on what you observe in the natural as true, such as how well you are keeping the works of the law] is death, but to [live by focusing your mind on what God has done for you in Jesus as true] is life and peace. Because the [mind that focuses on what you observe in the natural as true, such as how well you are keeping the works of the law] will see God as an enemy, for it will observe that it is not subject to the law of God, nor indeed can it be. So then, those who [live by focusing their mind on what they observe in the natural, such as how well they are keeping the works of the law] cannot please God.* I encourage you to use this lens to reread all of Romans 8. That chapter of the Bible will take on an entirely powerful new meaning for you.

Finally, applying this same interpretative mechanism to the very popular Galatians 5:16-25, we see Paul beginning to lay the foundation for how a believer, by living according to the truth of the gospel, would accomplish what they could never have done by attempting to keep the law.

Galatians 5:16 would now read as *"Live as though what God has done for you in Jesus is true, and you shall not fulfill the sinful lusts that come from living as if what you observe in the natural, such as how well you keep the laws, is true...."*

Galatians 5:17 would read: *"For what you want when you live as if what you observe in your natural life, such as how well you are keeping the laws of God is true, is against what you would want if you lived as if what God has done for you in Jesus were true...."*

Galatians 5:19 would read: *"the works that will manifest in your life if you are living as if what you see in the natural, such as how well you keep the laws of God, are adultery, fornication, uncleanness, lewdness...."*

Galatians 5:22 would then read: *"the fruit that will be produced in your life if you live as though all God has done for you in Jesus is true will be love, joy, peace...."*

And finally, Galatians 5:25 would read: *"If God has made you alive by what he did for you in Jesus in the realms of the Spirit, then live as if what God has done for you in Jesus is true...."*

Why does Paul make this assertion? Recall that in God's original plan, we were never supposed to take any action based on just what we observe through our natural senses. Rather, we were supposed to live dependent on what God, who is Spirit, reveals to us. I believe this was what the Tree of Life was to do for humankind in the garden of Eden. In other words, although man had his natural senses with which he was to operate in a natural, created universe, he was always to act and live from what God, who is Spirit, revealed to him. In other words, we were always supposed to live in the Spirit, and since the realm of the Spirit is unseen and unobservable to the natural senses, humankind had to live by faith in what God told them.

For example, when God said He had made man like God, in God's image and likeness, this was something that was done in the Spirit by a God who is Spirit. This act could not be observed with natural senses, but by "living in the Spirit"—that is, as if what God said he had done was indeed true, man would have come to experience that indeed he was like God and made in God's image and likeness. But when Adam and Eve in the garden disobeyed God and ate from the "Tree of the knowledge of good and evil," they chose the information coming to them via their natural senses above what God had declared to them as true in the Spirit (Genesis 3:1-,7). They lived as if the knowledge they obtained from what they observed in the natural was true, ignoring what God had told them. They chose the "works of the law," the things they could touch, taste, smell, hear, and feel to inform them about what was true rather than the "hearing of faith"—that is, that they had heard from God. They ate

Living in the Flesh versus Living in the Spirit

the fruit to be like God, this after God told them that they were like him already, made in God's image and likeness! They walked in the flesh and sinned, not because they broke some rule, but because they were in rebellion to the revealed word of God. They acted independently of God's Spirit. The "flesh," therefore, is simply relying on or going by your natural senses or observations independent of God's spirit. Put another way, whenever you walk by sight rather than by faith, you are walking in the flesh. It does not matter if what you did was actually "good." If you did it because of what you observed in the natural instead of what God has said in the Spirit, you have walked in the flesh.

> We experience death when we walk in the flesh. We experience life when we walk in the Spirit.

So we see that when Paul says that we receive salvation by faith, we are choosing to walk in the Spirit, to agree with God that what He said He has done for us in Jesus is true. In essence, we are acting contrary to how our forefathers, Adam and Eve, acted. To be lost, man lived in the flesh — he acted based on what he perceived in the natural; he doubted what God had said was true in the Spirit. To receive salvation, we must walk in the Spirit. We must accept what God has said is true in the Spirit (that is, God has saved you through Jesus) as true, despite what we perceive in the natural.

Once we understand this, we begin to see how consistent the scriptures are and how, although different metaphors are used, the Lord is essentially speaking to us about the same thing. For example, in Galatians 3, Paul says you are foolish if, after you have begun in the Spirit (which is being saved by faith), you now trying to become mature as a Christian or increase in God's acceptance of you by looking at how well you are doing in the natural (such as how well you are keeping the laws). You are repeating the very same actions of Adam and Eve, which caused them to fall in the first place; you are living in the flesh. In 2 Corinthians 5:7, Paul says we walk by faith (that is, we live in the Spirit; or by believing that what God says He has done for us in Jesus is true) and not by sight (such as how well we are keeping the law or by what we observe in the natural). In John 15:4, Jesus says, "abide in me," which means live as though when God says he has placed you in Jesus, you are. This is the same thing as living by faith or walking in the Spirit. On the other hand, Jesus says: "he that abides not in me, is cast out..." He means he that ignores what God says he has done for you in Jesus and chooses instead to live by what he observes in the natural, such as how well he keeps the works of the law. So you see how when Paul says, "walk in the Spirit" to bear the fruit of the Spirit, and Jesus says "abide in me" in order to be fruitful, they are speaking of the same thing — which is, "live as though what God said he has done for you in Jesus is true."

Going back to our text in Galatians 3, we see what Paul is communicating under the inspiration of the Holy Spirit. We are living in the flesh if we preach or minister Holy Ghost baptism, step out to preach the gospel, step out to pray for the sick, or work miracles ONLY after we have "worked on ourselves," "paid the price," "cleansed ourselves," "for-

Living in the Flesh versus Living in the Spirit 77

tified ourselves"—or whatever spiritual terminology we use to describe some natural thing we feel we must do to ask God to move in our lives. I am not against doing these things; neither is Paul against them. But we must not do them to earn us the approval or blessings of God. Rather, we should do them as things that would help us quit observing how we are doing in the natural (i.e., living in the flesh) so we can live more according to what God said He did for us (i.e., living in the Spirit).

We are living in the flesh if we think that it is by our good efforts, prayers, activities, way of dressing, or whatever—that we are "filled with the Holy Spirit," "get more of the Holy Spirit," or "become more anointed." "Walking in the Spirit" means stepping out in faith to minister Holy Ghost baptism or praying for people whether we feel adequate or not. We do this knowing that God has transformed us in the Spirit and accepts us 100 percent, all the time, not because of our efforts, but because of what God did for us in Jesus. It is acting according to the truth of the gospel we hear, the hearing of faith, and keeping our eyes on Jesus, not on ourselves. Again, are positive efforts good? Yes, they are, but only to the extent that they help us to grow in our faith or to help us receive more of what God has already done. They are of no use in getting God to do more for us, or to earn anything from God! Our efforts help us, not God. God does not need our help with something He has ALREADY done!

Therefore, beloved, you can see more manifestation of God than you see now in your academics, your relationships, your business, your professional life, or in your ministry. All you need to do is to step out in faith and announce what God has done for you and for all people already in Jesus. As you do so, heal the sick, raise the dead, cleanse the lepers, and cast out demons (Matthew 10:7-8). Go for opportunities and challenges that may seem too big for you to perform if you looked at only the natural. Walk in the spirit, not in the flesh. You do not need to be more anointed than you are right now; God has anointed you already with the fullness of the Spirit of Jesus. This is true, regardless of what you are observing in the natural world right now. God does not need to give you more. He does not have any more to give because He has already given you all. In the Spirit, you have it all—all things that pertain to life and godliness (2 Peter 1:3). So, walk in the Spirit! Receive more of all that has been given to you right now! Step out in faith! The weakest among us can perform the mightiest of acts—it is not who we are in the flesh that matters, but who we are in the Spirit—and who we are in the spirit is settled forever in Jesus. As we shall see in the next chapter, as God told Abraham, "it is set as the stars in the sky" (Hebrews 11:11-13)!

 DEEPENING YOUR UNDERSTANDING

What does this all mean?

- Why do Christians often think that, although the gospel saves them, growth comes by applying biblical principles or keeping the works of the law in various areas of their lives?

- Why do you think Paul insists that since we did not

begin in the flesh (by keeping the law), it is foolish to think we could mature in the flesh (by keeping the law)?

- Why is it that if we began in the Spirit (i.e., by faith in Jesus alone), we could only grow in the Spirit (i.e., by faith in Jesus alone)? How would this effort look if we tried a practical approach?

- Is it consistent to tell a sinner before he is saved, "God loves and accepts you in Jesus—no matter what you may have done" and then, after they are saved, our message changes to "God loves and accepts you—as long as you continue to be of good behavior"?

- Many people believe that the gospel is for sinners and that deep, spiritual stuff that produces spiritual growth is now what we need to grow. How can someone who is saved by the gospel grow by applying the gospel to every area of life?

APPLYING WHAT YOU HAVE LEARNED

Now, what do I do?

- Your human body is not evil. Living from it is (i.e., living in the flesh). What can you do to help you live less in your flesh and more in the Spirit?

- Paul is not against spiritual disciplines (fasting, prayers, silence, submission, forgiveness, and so on). He is against faith in spiritual disciplines. What can you do so that while you perform these disciplines, your faith remains in God — not in your good efforts?

- Share practical solutions. How can a Christian struggling with anger or unforgiveness grow as a Christian by applying the gospel (what God has done for him or her in Jesus) in that area of his or her life?

CHAPTER 6

Faith in A Faithful God

Therefore He who supplies the Spirit to you and works miracles among you, does He do it by the works of the law, or by the hearing of faith? just as Abraham "believed God, and it was accounted to him for righteousness." Therefore know that only those who are of faith are sons of Abraham. And the Scripture, foreseeing that God would justify the Gentiles by faith, preached the gospel to Abraham beforehand, saying, "In you, all the nations shall be blessed." So then those who are of faith are blessed with believing Abraham (Galatians 3:5–9, NKJV).

We ended the last chapter by asserting that to walk in the Spirit or abide in Christ, whatever metaphor we use, essentially means to walk and live by faith that what God has said is true is really true. This we must do, especially when everything around us seems to suggest that it is not so. There is no story in the Bible that better encapsulates this than the story of Abram described in Genesis 15. Paul refers to it in the verses we are considering. Although this is a story most of us are familiar with, it is worth going back to Genesis 15 and reading the account again to refresh our memories.

The story begins in Genesis 11:27–32. As the long genealogy of Shem, one of Noah's sons, comes to an end, we find an odd account of a man called Terah leaving his hometown, the cosmopolitan and prosperous city of Ur, which, at that time, was the center of world civilization. Terah left Ur with his sons Abram and Nahor and their wives. Note that the Bible says that they left "to go to the land of Canaan." Contrary to popular belief, when they left Ur, they knew their ultimate destination. They may not have known precisely where in Canaan they were to settle, but they knew it was Canaan. However, when you get to Genesis 12:1, after Terah dies halfway into the migration, the Bible says, "... now the Lord *had* said to Abram, get out of your country, from your family, and from your father's house, to a land that I will show you." If you compare this verse with other Bible passages — such as Genesis 15:7, Acts 7:2-4, and Joshua 24:3, you realize that although all of Terah's family left Ur, it was only Abram whom God called. To what had God called Abram? It was more than to occupy a piece of real estate. He was called because of what God had already planned to do through Abram. God called him out of a morally bankrupt, polytheistic lifestyle into a monotheistic faith and lifestyle. This call meant a radical change in Abram's life — including uprooting him from the only world and life he knew, to begin anew in the uncertain world of Canaan.

In Genesis 12, therefore, Abram left his home and country for an unknown destination, on the back of a promise from God that He would give him a family through which the whole world would be blessed and saved. Put another way, God called Abraham to "walk in the Spirit" — to live as though what God had said about him was true. In taking his father and extended family along, Abram did not fully walk according to the Spirit, and this almost torpedoed his experience of what God had done. As we read on, we find this pattern repeating itself over and over again. This man Abram, on his journey of faith with God, struggled with his doubts and fears, often did not walk in the Spirit (i.e., live by faith) but walked in the flesh. While he was responding to God as best he could, he was constantly halting and making mistakes. He would stop briefly in Damascus, then leave to continue to Canaan. When a famine arose, he rushed to Egypt to save his life. And in Egypt, he lied to save his skin. In the process, he risked the life of his wife, Sarai.

By the time we get to Genesis 15, after several years of seemingly aimless wanderings, famine, endangered life in Egypt, war with kings, and the pain of a childless marriage, Abraham comes to God, confused, tired, weary, and about to give up. In a way, Abraham feels as though he has failed God, that he let God down somehow. Had he obeyed enough? Was the journey to Egypt and his lie there too costly a mistake? Assailed by his doubts, he tells God to end the plan with him and restart it with Eliezer, one of his servants. But we see a wonderful thing happen in this story. God was not mad at Abraham for this show of doubt, fear, and unbelief. Instead, God did two things to demonstrate to Abraham that God's salvation and what God had done were not dependent on Abraham's performance.

First, He took him out and showed him the stars and said to him, "so shall thy seed be!" Alleluia. In other words, God said to Abraham: "the promise of your seed is my promise to you that through you and your family, the One who would come so that the whole world is blessed and delivered" is just like the stars. As you did not make the stars and cause them to suspend so gloriously in the darkness of the night, so also you cannot make this thing happen! Only I can make it happen! Not only that, you cannot make it happen, just as you do not contribute anything to the making of the stars, you also cannot contribute anything to making this thing I have promised you happen!

> Just as we did not contribute anything to the making of the stars, so also do we not contribute anything to the accomplishment of the promises of God.

Please pause for a moment to reflect on the breathtaking message God was delivering to Abraham? How many times have we heard statements like "heaven helps those who help themselves"? Here is God telling Abraham: "this is going to be 100 percent heaven and 0 percent you! It does not matter how many missteps you take along the way", God said, "I have already made this happen, and you have no contribution to make to it because you have nothing to contribute." And if there was ever a doubt about this, both Abram and Sarai were unable to have children! Even if they wanted to contribute, they could not. Thank heavens God had already settled it, like the stars!

Can you imagine the implications if Abram and Sarai were needed to make this happen? Can you imagine what it would have meant if Abram had to be fully and completely obedient to God for this promise of God to come to pass? Imagine if it was one of those things where Abram's input was needed, then Abram and all of humanity would be doomed! Not only had Abram made so many mistakes and missteps, but he and his wife were also infertile! This is why we must be so glad that our blessings, our salvation, our victory, our success—cannot be dependent on anything we can contribute, because if it is, then we are completely doomed.

But I also believe that God may have even had even more to tell Abram when He pointed the stars to him. Now, Abram may not have known this, but we who live in these last days and have the benefit of science can appreciate this even more. Scientists measure the distance between the stars and other intergalactic bodies in light-years. Light-years means the distance light will travel in one year. Scientists tell us that the nearest star to Earth is the Proxima Centauri and is about four light-years away. When you stand outside at night and gaze upon the star known as the Proxima Centauri, you are not looking at the light coming from that star at that moment. Rather, you are looking at the light that had been emitted by that star four light-years ago. A human spaceship would take 73,000 years to get to the Proxima Centauri. The Milky Way Galaxy, in which our Sun and all the stars we see at night reside, spans 100,000 light-years from one end to the other. This means that several of the stars you are looking at on any starry night were light emitted over 100,000 thousand light-years ago!

So, there was something else God was saying to Abram

when He pointed him to the stars: "not only are you not going to be able to contribute to the fulfillment of my promise, but also, just like the stars, I have already done it. The announcement of the promise that you hear today is not because the promise is going to be done today; the promise has already been done! Your seed has already happened! Billions of years ago in eternity, before you even showed up, Abram—I set your seed like I set the stars in the sky! Alleluia!"

No wonder the Bible says, "And Abraham believed God, and God credited him with, lodged in his account, righteousness" (Galatians 3:6). God declared an unrighteous man righteous, accepted an outsider into the family of God, simply because that man could believe that what God had done in the Spirit was true! Jesus, speaking of this event in John 8:56, says: "Abraham rejoiced to see My day; and he saw it and was glad."

But God did not stop there. He proceeded to swear an oath and cut a covenant with Abraham. In ancient times when people cut a covenant, they would take an animal and cut it into two halves. Standing in the midst of the butchered animal, they will swear an oath saying, "may I be cut into pieces like this animal if I break this covenant." God, willing to assure Abraham of his commitment to the Promise, asked Abraham to take some animals and cut them into pieces and lay them on a rock as Abraham would have done if he wanted to enter into a covenant. The Bible says in Genesis 15:17-18 that while Abraham slept, God passed through those pieces of cut animals as a burning lamp and then proceeded to swear an oath to Abraham. Note that God alone passed through the midst of the cut animals and God alone swore an oath at this covenant ceremony. In other words, God was saying to Abraham, "if I need to, I will cut myself in pieces to ensure that I bless you and that my promise comes to pass that through your seed, you and the rest of the world would be blessed and saved!"

> Two thousand years ago, on the cross of Calvary, in Jesus, God cut Himself into pieces, in order to secure the salvation of all people.

Two thousand years ago, on the cross of Calvary, God indeed cut himself into pieces in Jesus to secure the salvation of all people. In Jesus, our God was bruised, broken, and torn apart as He bore the sins of the whole world—past, present, and future—to make sure that the whole world is reconciled to God. So if you think about it, Abraham was saved and made righteous in the same way we are saved and made righteous. While he looked forward to the Lamb of God who was to be slain, we are looking backward to the Lamb Who was slain. No wonder Paul asked the Galatians—who has bewitched you...before whose eyes Jesus Christ was portrayed as crucified! May you see it today and be glad like Abraham all those years ago.

And when I think, that God, his Son not sparing,
Sent him to die, I scarce can take it in,
That on the cross, my burden gladly bearing,
He bled and died to take away my sin.

Then sings my soul, my Savior God, to thee:
How great thou art! How great thou art!
Then sings my soul, my Savior God, to thee:
How great thou art! How great thou art!
(Hymn, "How Great Thou Art" by Stuart K. Hine, 1931)

DEEPENING YOUR UNDERSTANDING

What does this all mean?

- What does it mean that Abraham's faith was credited? On what basis does God credit righteousness to Abraham? How is Abraham's saving faith a model for us?

- If faith is believing that what God has done is true and then deciding to live as though it were true, what exactly did Abraham believe about God that was credited to him as righteousness?

- How can God call the unrighteous righteous? Isn't this contrary to the holiness and righteousness of God?

APPLYING WHAT YOU'VE LEARNED

Now, what do I do?

- When Abraham saw how God could go to any extent— including crucifixion—not to lose him, Abraham was ready to give up all for God. This included his foreskin (circumcision) and even Isaac, the son of

Faith in A Faithful God

his love for Sarah. Do you feel such compulsion with God? Having seen how far God has gone for you, do you feel a compulsion to go far for Him, too?

- Do you feel that there is nothing you cannot give up for this God who has given up all for you? What can you do to feel and see God's love for you as Abraham saw it—and rejoice?

CHAPTER 7
Our Adoption as Sons And Daughters

Even so we, when we were children, were in bondage under the elements of the world. But when the fullness of the time had come, God sent forth His Son, born of a woman, born under the law, to redeem those who were under the law, that we might receive the adoption as sons. And because you are sons, God has sent forth the Spirit of His Son into your hearts, crying out, "Abba, Father!" Therefore you are no longer a slave but a son, and if a son, then an heir of God through Christ (Galatians 4:3–7, NKJV).

To me, these verses are perhaps some of the most precious verses in the book of Galatians. While this is not the main point of the book, it appears as if in this one place, Paul, for a moment, lays aside his frustrations with the Galatians to help them see the big picture. The core truth of the gospel is that God, because of His love for us, sent Jesus His Son to perform two works of grace for all who believe. First, Jesus came to redeem those who, under the law, were condemned to death and separation from God by that law. Secondly, at the same time, Jesus gave those whom He redeemed their adoption papers into the family of God as Sons of God so that they now have the Spirit of the Son God and are now heirs of the Almighty God.

Let's look at the first work of grace: redemption from the condemnation we deserved under the law. Under the law, every single human is condemned to death and eternal separation from God. As we shall soon see, the law was never given as the way for a man to be accepted with God. The purpose of the law was to show us and bring us the awareness of our sinful nature through our constant acts of sin and disobedience to the law (Romans 3:19-20; 7:8). It is through the law that we come to know that we are sinners by nature. This means that we are not sinners because we sin. We sin because we are sinners. And as a result of our sinfulness, death was the destiny of us all. But the Bible says that God, through His grace and because of His love for us, stepped in to pay the debt of death we owed as a result of our sin (2 Corinthians 5:19-21). Beloved, the consequences of all your sins have been paid for, the debt you owed for sinning. Therefore you have been redeemed from (fully paid for) every requirement and consequence your sins deserve!

> The consequences of all your sins – past, present and future – have all been paid for. You have been redeemed from every requirement and consequence your sins deserve.

Most people struggle with this truth of the gospel that God, through the death of Jesus, has paid for all our sins — past, present, and future. On the one hand, people struggle with understanding the fact that God "forgiving our sins" means God has taken on the consequence of their sins on their behalf. The question often asked is: why does God not just go ahead and forgive sins so that there is no more need for punishment or payment for the sins? Why did God, through Jesus, have to take on our sins Himself in order for us to be "forgiven"? The root of this struggle comes from a wrong view of God as "the God who punishes people for their sins." The Bible, especially in New Testament, actually portrays a radically different view of God. Rather than God being presented as the One who metes out death to the sinner, He is instead the One who has come to rescue the sinner from the death that their sin deserves, and that is also the consequence of that sin. Jesus reveals to us not a God who punishes sinners but One who comes to rescue sinners. This is why Romans 6:23 makes it clear that "the wages of sin is death." It is not the wages that God pays for sinning but the wages we get from sin. Death, i.e., loss of life and all its attendant ill, is what we deserve for sin in our lives. In the Bible, sin, in addition to being an act of rebellion against God, is also depicted as a personality, a mindset that is in acute rebellion against God. We do not only do wrong; we do wrong because we are in rebellion against God. The "personality of sin" in us, that "rebel" in us that lives and walks in rebellion against God, what Paul calls "the man or person of sin," is what draws us to acts of rebellion against God or sin. The moment we align with this rebel, "sin," we disconnect or become unaligned with God, the God who is LIFE and in whom LIFE exists. As a result, death, extinction of life, is the natural consequence of this alignment with rebellion. It is not God but sin that punishes us for sinning. This is why it is often said that "people are not punished for their sins as much as they are punished by them." When sin or rebellion against God entered our universe, death entered also and spread to all people. Paul says, "through the disobedience (rebellion) of one man, sin entered and death through sin" (Romans 5:19), but through the obedience of one man, Life entered and counteracted the effect of the sin-bred death in us. God came to rescue us by bearing the consequences of our sin and rebellion. Put another way, because God already forgave us of our sins, and He came to bear the consequences for us.

The other aspect of this gospel truth that people struggle with is that God has taken on himself and fully paid the debt for ALL our sins, past, present, and future. How can God take on the consequences of the sin that I have not yet committed? And if it is so, does this mean I can now go ahead and commit any sin I want, knowing that God has already borne the consequences for it? Let's start with the fact that God has paid for all your sins, past, present, and future. The fact is, at the time God paid for all our sins in Jesus, even the sins you call "past sins" today were all still in the future! In other words, if God cannot pay for sins before you commit them, then even the sins you claim are in the past would not have been paid for, because they were all in the future when Jesus died on the cross to pay for them. In Hebrews 10:14, the Bible says: "for, by ONE sacrifice, he has made perfect forever those whom He has made holy..."! Also in Hebrews 9:26-27, the Bible says that "as a man will die once for all the sins he will ever commit (past, present, and future) — so also Jesus, the Eternal

Son of God, died once for all your sins (past, present, and future). Death is the consequence of ALL sin. And when God died for us and as us, we in God, now have the consequence of all our sins paid for by God and in God!

But God did not stop there. Redemption from the evil consequences of our sinfulness was not all that God did for us through Jesus. Paul says God's Son proceeded to give us the adoption as sons and daughters, an adoption process that began when we were born of the Spirit of God when we received the Spirit of God's Son (which carries the life of the Son—James 2:26). Through this action, we become "begotten of God"—hence the word "born again." We become heirs of God, that is, inheritors of the very nature of God Himself. And everything that belongs to God now belongs to us as His beloved sons and daughters. That is to say, through His death and resurrection, Jesus did not only take on your sins and die in your place; you also took on His sinless life, the uncorrupted, fully righteous life of the Son of God.

Paul, describing this in 2 Corinthians 5:21, paints a picture of a Great Exchange. He who knew no sin took your sins and paid the price for your sins, i.e., death and separation from God, and you who knew no righteousness took the righteousness of Jesus, which Paul calls "the righteousness of God." As a result, every blessing, every reward, and every good thing Jesus ought to have received because He was a Son, all the blessings to Him who is in right-standing with God, is now yours who according to the law, was unrighteous before God! You are now a child of God and have inherited that which should have gone to Him (Jesus), who was righteous in the eyes of the law.

Our Adoption as Sons And Daughters 95

As a child of God and co-heir with Jesus, Christ's sinless life has become yours, just as your sinful life became His. Just as He took the punishment for all your sins, you now get all the rewards and blessings for His keeping all the law. Just as your sin puts Christ on the cross, so also his fulfilling of the law 100 percent puts you into God's family and what makes the life of God available to you. Christ fulfilled all the law and yet died, contrary to the law (Ezekiel 18:10). Therefore, He died to the law because the law was unable to save Him, even though He kept all its provisions! So also you who breaks all the law (remember that if you break just one, you have broken all — see James 2:10) will yet live and be blessed, contrary to the law because, in Christ, you too who are dead to the law will not be condemned by it. All of this is what you inherit as an heir of God — a Son of God who has received an inheritance (something another person has worked for all their life that becomes yours simply by birth, not by your effort).

To me, this second aspect of God's work of grace in our lives is something we have not paid enough attention to in the church. There seems to be a lot of emphasis on what was taken away (our sins) but not as much emphasis on what we received at the same time our sins were taken away. To me, one story in the Bible that depicts the importance of grasping this truth of what we gain because we are now "sons of God" is found in the story of Job.

In Job 1, we are given the account of the gathering of the "sons of God." Some modern translations translate this to "angels." Other theologians hold the view that this is an Old Testament way of describing a meeting of the Godhead, but the exact nature of who these persons are is a mystery. In

Job 1:6, the Bible says, "…and Satan also came for that meeting." For a long time, it puzzled me how the vile, evil, and wicked Satan could gain access to such a sacred gathering of the sons of God, and it seemed I was not the only one who was puzzled, as the Bible says in Job 1:7 that the Lord asked Satan "where have you come from?" To which the devil replied, "From roaming throughout the earth, going back and forth on it." This passage of the scriptures puzzled me until one day, at a Bible study in a church I was visiting, my eyes were opened to see what was going on here. It is important to go back to Genesis to understand this fully.

In Genesis 1, the Bible says that when God made man, He gave man full dominion and authority over all created universe. The Bible in Luke 3:38 called Adam "the son of God," and it was Adam and his descendants that God had given the responsibility to "roam throughout the earth, going back and forth on it" and bringing about dominion and the glory of God on the earth. It was this same Adam who handed over his title papers to the earth and his position as "son of God" to Satan when he yielded to the devil and disobeyed God. Therefore; when God was having a meeting of the Sons of God, rather than Adam or Man's representative to be in this meeting, Satan, the usurper, came into this meeting, using the papers/authority he usurped from Adam and as you can see from that story, it was this authority that gave him the ability to inflict harm and damage on Job and his family!

But God be praised, Alleluia! Paul says that Jesus came and defeated Satan, snatched from him our authority which he stole and gave it back to us! Now we who are in Jesus

Our Adoption as Sons And Daughters

are "the sons of God." Now no longer does Satan have a place in the meeting of the sons and daughters of God; we too now have access to that meeting in Jesus! Now we can go, as Satan did in Job, and rather than bringing death and destruction, we can bring life, healing, and joy. We are sons and daughters of God; we can roam the face of the universe and restore life where the enemy traveled and brought death. We are the sons and daughters of God; we can intercede for people's lives and livelihoods rather than intercede for their destruction. It is time for us to arise and take our place in our Father's house as his children.

> "The core truth of the gospel is that Almighty God has chosen to be the Father of everyone who believes in Jesus... If you know God in every other way but Father, you are not a Christian. He has given all who believe in Him the right to call him Father." – Dr. Cosmas Ilechukwu

As I conclude this chapter, I remember a message Dr. Cosmas Ilechukwu, General Overseer of Charismatic Renewal Ministries, gave when he visited our church a few years back:

"The core truth of the gospel is that Almighty God has chosen to be the Father of everyone who believes in Jesus. The Fatherhood of God underlines the redemptive work of the Lord Jesus. He redeemed us that God would call us "sons," and we may come to know Him and relate with Him as Father. Actualizing the Father-

hood of God is the ultimate goal of our faith, and God has given you His Holy Spirit to confirm that you are indeed his Son and to help you actualize the Fatherhood of God in your life. This way, you will not live your Christian life as an orphan. There is no greater blessing than to come under the fatherly influence of the Almighty Father. If you know God in every other way but Father, you are not a Christian. He has given all who believe in Him the right to call him Father. If Jesus is your Savior, then His Father is your Father. If Jesus's Father is your Father – then you are co-heirs with Jesus of EVERYTHING that God has. The enemy does not want us to know what these things are, and he keeps us running around with religious notions of God. I challenge you today to begin to relate with God as your Father." Alleluia!

DEEPENING YOUR UNDERSTANDING

What does this mean?

- What do you understand by Paul's statement in 2 Corinthians 5:19 that God reconciled the world to Himself by not counting their sins against them? Is it only the sins of those who believe that are not counted? How many sins are not counted? Is it just past sins, or all sins ever committed?

- How would your dying with Jesus on the cross lead to salvation from your sins? If in Jesus you have died for your sins, can you die again for the same sins?

- Compare and contrast Romans 8:12-17 with Galatians 4:4-7. Is Paul presenting the same truth in different ways? Or, are these two different truths and experiences? If Paul is presenting the same truth, how could this give us a clearer meaning of what it means to "walk in the flesh" versus "walking in" or "being led by the Spirit"?

APPLYING WHAT YOU HAVE LEARNED

Now, what do I do?

- Make a list of all the things you have inherited NOW because God made Jesus a sinner for you and made you a son or daughter in His stead? What can you do today to experience more of this in your life?

- It is appointed unto man once to die for all their sins (See Hebrews 9:27). You are dead with Jesus on the cross. What can you do so that you are no longer constantly living under the condemnation of your sin but in the freedom from guilt that Christ has purchased for you?

- If you are now a son or daughter of God by God's grace, how should you now live your life? If you now have the life of Jesus, what should you now do with that life? If you are not doing this, is it because you do not know how to change your life — or is it because you do not want to? If you want to live your life differently, what can you do to live out the life of Jesus — which you now have?

CHAPTER 8
The Lawful Use of the Law

But then, indeed, when you did not know God, you served those which by nature are not gods. But now after you have known God, or rather are known by God, how is it that you turn again to the weak and beggarly elements, to which you desire again to be in bondage? You observe days and months and seasons and years. I am afraid for you, lest I have labored for you in vain (Galatians 4:8–11 NKJV).

What purpose then does the law serve? It was added because of transgressions, till the Seed should come to whom the promise was made; and it was appointed through angels by the hand of a mediator. Now a mediator does not mediate for one only, but God is one. Is the law then against the promises of God? Certainly not! For if there had been a law given which could have given life, truly righteousness would have been by the law. But the Scripture has confined all under sin, that the promise by faith in Jesus Christ might be given to those who believe. But before faith came, we were kept under guard by the law, kept for the faith which would afterward be revealed. Therefore the law was our tutor to bring us to Christ, that we might be justified by faith. But after faith has come, we are no longer under a tutor (Galatians 3:19–25 NKJV).

If we do not receive salvation (i.e., reconciliation with our Father God and entrance into the Divine family) by keeping the law but by faith alone in what God has done for us through Jesus, of what use then is the law? Are Christians thus expected to be lawless and without laws? God forbid! First, Paul tells us that the chief and proper use of the law is to "tutor" the sinner to Christ the Savior. No one demonstrated this proper use of the law more than Jesus Himself. We see this in Mark 10:17-27 and Matthew 19:16-26. A rich young ruler came to Jesus feeling good about his religious achievement and his own goodness. Jesus used the law to prove to this young man that, indeed, no one was good enough to receive eternal life. After the young man claimed that he had kept all the commandments Jesus listed, Jesus used the law to prove to him that he did not measure up to God's holiness. He asked the young ruler to sell all his property, give the money to the poor, and follow Jesus. The man was not willing to follow the Lord if that meant he must give up his wealth.

> There is a lawful use of the law. There is also an unlawful use of the law. Any attempt to use the law as basis of righteousness or acceptance with God is an unlawful use of the law.

Jesus used this to show this young man that, despite what he thought of himself, he was breaking the two greatest commandments. First, he did not love his neighbor as himself. Secondly, he did not love the Lord with all his heart. He loved himself and his money more. Therefore, far from keeping all the commandments as he had claimed, the man was a sinner like everyone else. Jesus used the law to prove it. If the man had loved God and other people more than he did his property, he would have been willing to give up his wealth in the service of God and humankind. However, he had made an idol of his wealth; he loved it more than God, and he loved himself more than he loved others. With surgical precision, Jesus used the law to expose the greed in the man's heart—greed that the man did not even suspect he had. Jesus used the law to prove to this young man that indeed there was none good but God (Matthew 19:17).

This is why the law was given; not to make one righteous, but to show one a transgressor, a sinner (Galatians 3:19), to make sin exceedingly sinful and declare us all sinners (Romans 7:13; Galatians 3:2). The law was given to show that ONLY by perfectly keeping ALL the law could one be saved—and at the same time show that we could NEVER meet this righteous requirement of the law, and hence, all our efforts to please God are worthless. The law was given to show that we, in ourselves, were not good, and we were not righteous. We were cursed and completely deserving of judgment (Galatians 3:10-14). This is the only lawful use of the law when it comes to someone who has yet to receive God's salvation, which comes by faith in Jesus. Any other use of the law by such a person is an illegal or unlawful use of the law, and we know that the law is good if one uses it lawfully (1 Timothy 1:8).

Another place we see the proper or lawful use of the law is in Jesus's Sermon on the Mount found in Matthew 5, 6, and 7. A traditional way of viewing these Scripture passages suggests that Jesus came to tighten the law His followers were expected to keep. Jesus, as the teaching goes, came to show His followers that "you should not kill" actually includes hating your brother; or that you have already broken the commandment not to commit adultery simply by looking at a woman or man lustfully. And so, the teaching goes, Jesus came to strengthen, expatiate, and fully explain the law. Reading it this way, while not entirely inaccurate, completely misses the point of Jesus's entire sermon. A few points are often necessary to establish and fully understand and appreciate what Jesus was trying to achieve with his Sermon on the Mount.

The first thing is to remember that this was a sermon Jesus preached, not a blog post or newspaper article. As a result, like every sermon, Jesus had an objective that He hoped his sermon would achieve. He had a main point that He was trying to drive home to help Him achieve His objective. He also added supporting points to His main point. Jesus also used illustrations and examples to try to get His point across to His listeners. Let's start with Jesus's objective: what was He trying to achieve? Remember that Jesus was essentially the last prophet of the Old Testament and the first prophet of the New Testament. Jesus came to do away with the old so that the new may come. Jesus, who was born under the law and the Old Testament, had to convince the people of His time of the futility and failure of the Old Testament. Then they could turn to Him—the Author and Finisher of the New Testament. To do this, His primary goal was to show the people the weakness of the law and the reasons why it was not good enough to save them.

Once you approach the Sermon on the Mount—and indeed, most of Jesus's teachings—this way, the scales drop off, and the entire passages come alive. The anchor verse, where Jesus stated His main point, can be found in Matthew 5:20. In that verse, Jesus said, "unless your righteousness exceeds that of the scribes and Pharisees, you cannot in anywise enter life." This statement of Jesus must have shocked his listeners. The Pharisees were the most outwardly righteous people in Israel. They were the most stringent followers of the law. That was an incredulous statement! I can almost see someone raise his voice to Jesus and say, "Rabbi, can you please explain? That simply makes no sense." Jesus then goes ahead to show, through the law, how the righteousness of the Pharisees and the scribes fell short of the will of God.

For example, Jesus says, how are you different from a murderer if you say you are righteous and have never committed murder but harbor the same anger and contempt that one must have in order to commit murder? How are you different from an adulterer or fornicator when you are dominated by the same sexual lust that drives a man or woman to infidelity in their marriage? You say you are not an adulterer but can't you see that your divorcing your wife (even though it was done according to the law of Moses) in other to marry the next hot woman you come across is simply a manifestation of lust in your heart? Can't you see you are yet an adulterer? How are you different from the tax collectors and sinners if you love only those who love you and hate those who hate you? And on and on Jesus went, tearing down the "righteousness" based on keeping the law (the righteousness of the Pharisees) whereas the heart of the person keeping the law is not right with God. And He did this using the law! This is the proper and lawful use of the law.

> Faith in Jesus as Savior, by necessity, implies faith in yourself as a sinner in desperate need of a Savior.

Why is this use of the law important? It is important because until a person fully acknowledges that he or she is a sinner in desperate need of a Savior, such a person cannot fully and truly place all their faith in Jesus to be saved. It is impossible to truly, wholly, and fully put your faith in Jesus as the only means of your salvation until and unless you have lost all faith in yourself and have come to fully believe that you are a sinner in desperate need of a Savior. Faith in Jesus, by necessity, includes faith in yourself as a sinner in desperate need of a Savior. This is why faith in Jesus includes repentance—not just turning away from sin, but also turning away from your good efforts as the basis of your acceptance with God. The tax collector and the Pharisee needed to repent and come to Jesus. The tax collector repents for his outright breaking of God's laws. The Pharisee repents for his reason for keeping God's law. As someone said, we contribute nothing to our salvation because we have nothing to contribute except sin. The law is what proves this to us. This is the chief and proper use of the law.

In his seminal work *Mere Christianity*, English author and

scholar C. S. Lewis describes this proper use of the law well. In his chapter on faith, Lewis talks about how one can come to what we call "saving faith" — or faith in the finished work of Jesus as the basis of salvation. According to Lewis, it is impossible for a man to come to saving faith without first experiencing deep humility. One way to get there, Lewis says, is for a person to commit to making a serious attempt to practice Christian virtues; in our case, keep the law. For example, make a serious attempt to love your neighbor as yourself by seeking to always treat everyone you meet — good, bad, or ugly — the same way you would love to be treated; or maybe make a serious attempt not to commit sexual immorality in word, thought, or action; or perhaps try not to act in a hateful way toward anyone. Do not try for a week, Lewis says. Things often go swimmingly well in the first week. Try it for six weeks! By that time you have fallen back completely, or even fallen lower than the point one began from, this failed attempt to keep the law 100 percent reveals some truths about ourselves. Let's allow C. S. Lewis to speak for himself:

"No man knows how bad he is till he has tried very hard to be good. A silly idea is current that good people do not know what temptation means. This is an obvious lie. Only those who try to resist temptation know how strong it is. After all, you find out the strength of the German army by fighting against it, not by giving in. You find out the strength of a wind by trying to walk against it, not by lying down. A man who gives in to temptation after five minutes simply does not know what it would have been like an hour later. That is why bad people, in one sense, know very little about badness. They have lived a sheltered life by always giving

The Lawful Use of the Law

in. We never find out the strength of the evil impulse inside us until we try to fight it...The main thing we learn from a serious attempt to practice the Christian virtues (i.e., keeping the law) is that we fail. If there was any idea that God had set us a sort of exam and that we might get good marks by deserving them, that has to be wiped out. If there was any idea of a sort of bargain — any idea that we could perform our side of the contract and thus put God in our debts so that it was up to Him, in mere justice, to perform His side, that has to be wiped out. I think everyone who has some vague belief in God, until he becomes a Christian, has the idea of an exam, or of a bargain in his mind. The first result of real Christianity is to blow that idea into bits. When they find it blown into bits, some people think this means that Christianity is a failure and give up. They seem to imagine that God is very simple-minded! In fact, of course, He knows all about this. One of the very things Christianity was designed to do was to blow this idea to bits. God has been waiting for the moment at which you discover that there is no question of earning a pass mark in this exam, or putting Him in your debt." (C.S. Lewis, Mere Christianity, 1953)

This, my friends, is the reason why God gave the law — not so we can keep it, but to show, through our failure to keep it, that we are indeed in dire need of a Savior!

So now, if the law led me to Christ and now I am under grace and do not need to keep the law to be accepted by God because of God's grace, is the law no more relevant in my life? Having received Jesus as Savior and standing only on the merits of what He has done and having no more obligation to keep the law to earn the merits of God, do I then continue to sin because I am under grace? First, let me start by thanking you for asking that question. As someone once said, any presentation of the gospel message that does not naturally lead to this question is a faulty presentation of the gospel. This is the reason why in his Letter to the Church in Rome, Paul brought up this problem in various ways at least four times (Romans 3:5-8, Romans 3:31, Romans 6:1, and Romans 6:15)!

Let's take the question as posed in Romans 6:1. Leading up to Romans 6, in Romans 1, 2 and 3, Paul had established one fact: that ALL people, irrespective of their background, race, or religious persuasion, were sinners and worthy of consequences of their sin—i.e., death. Beginning in Romans 4, Paul begins to unveil God's rescue plan for humanity, what Paul called "the righteousness of God which is received by faith." Again, as he did when he wrote to the Galatians, Paul returned to how Abraham was saved, not by works, i.e., keeping any laws or rituals, but simply by believing. As we have already seen, God accepted Abraham (i.e., credited him with righteousness or accepted him as one of God's people) not because of what Abraham did, but because Abraham believed in what God did.

By the time we get to Romans 5, Paul begins to make a curious point: we should not find it unusual that we can be declared righteous and holy and acceptable to God because of the act of ANOTHER person! Why? Because we were made unrighteous, unholy, and sinful not because of our own actions but because of the act of another person - in this case, Adam. According to Paul: "Therefore just as through one man, sin (i.e., the evil rebellion against God, which we all have) entered the world, and death through sin, so that death spread to all men, because all men became sinners— even so, through one Man's righteous act, the gift (i.e., life) came to all men, resulting in justification of life! For as by one man's disobedience many were made sinners, so also by one Man's obedience many will be made righteous" (Romans 5:12, 18-19). The implication of this statement by Paul is tremendous. What this means is that a person will remain a sinner no matter how many good things they do because what makes this person a sinner is not what they do, but what another person (Adam) did. In the same way, a man will remain a SAINT no matter how many bad things he does because what makes him a SAINT is not what he does but what ANOTHER man (Jesus) did! Chew on that for a moment! If you are reading this book and you still have not placed ALL your confidence on the finished work of Jesus, you should put this book down and do so with all your heart. Unless you receive what Jesus has done as yours, NOTHING you do will reverse the tremendous evil you have inherited from Adam.

Continuing, you can now see why Paul's rhetorical question is the natural question that pops up: if having been made a saint and accepted by God because of what Jesus did and what I do or not do does not make me a sinner, shall I then continue to sin? (Romans 6:1). God forbid, Paul responds. Do you not know that since you are no longer under the law but under grace, that your life is now in an order higher than the law? Do you not know that although the law is no longer the basis for your being accepted by God, it is, however, the minimum standard by which your life must be lived if indeed it is true that you are now a saint?

For example, the law says, "love your neighbor as yourself." However, under grace, through the life of God that you have received, you get to love your neighbor as Jesus loved you. Therefore, you love your neighbor more than yourself. Under the law, you were required to bring 10 percent of your income as your tithes; but under grace, through the life of God in you, you get to give Him your all, just as He gave you His all. Under the law, God commanded you to love your brethren, but now under grace, you get to love even your enemies, just as Jesus loved you when you were His enemy. Don't you know that God's grace has given you the very nature of God Himself? So now you can be godly, i.e., live and act like God! Which means you get to live from love, the fruit of your new life in God, which is higher than God's laws to fallen humans. Can't you see that now you can be like your Father who does well, because it is good and because of love, and not out of a selfish desire to avoid punishment or reap a reward? This is a second and proper use of the law — not commands you have to obey to be blessed by God, but commands you choose to obey because you are filled with God's love; you are now like your Father who is in heaven.

It is important to note that in Romans 6, Paul did not address this issue by pointing back to the law or whipping out the Ten Commandments and showing them what laws to keep. Rather, Paul addressed this issue by pointing us back to "who we are already" in Christ. Paul goes on in Romans 6 to list several "know ye not…" statements, i.e., do you not know who you are? True Christianity does not send you back to the law to help you overcome sin; it points you to who you are in

Jesus. Paul says, "Do you not know that you are dead to sin? If this is true, how then can you continue to live in sin? Do you not know that you are baptized into Christ and therefore baptized into his death and resurrection! This means that the sinful man in you died on the cross with Jesus, and the new man of righteousness rose up with Jesus! How then, can you continue to live as if the sinful man is still there? Or do you not know that if you have died with Christ, you are now free from that sinful nature that ruled you and made you live as an enemy of God?" Paul goes on, making strong arguments why a man who is now in Christ—if indeed it is true that God has done all these mighty works in his life—should no longer sin but rather work out or show forth the truth of who he is right now in Christ Jesus. This is why, as Christians, we need to have a different attitude toward sin and temptation to sin. While for a sinner, sin and the temptation to sin is nothing more than a manifestation of who he is—a sinner; for the Christian, it is different. A Christian does not have a sin problem because God no longer relates with you based on whether you sin or not. He only relates with you based on what Jesus did. Therefore, as Christians, we must learn to begin to see the temptation to sin as nothing but an opportunity to manifest our true identities—who we are as sons and daughters of God.

Someone might ask: "My friends are living a life of sin and doing wrong daily, and the only reason why I have not joined them is that of my fear of God and of breaking His law. If you say that God no longer relates to me based on how well I am keeping or not keeping the law, what motivation then do I have for doing the right thing?" My response is this: if your fear of God's punishment is the only reason you have for not breaking His laws and living right, then you should go ahead and live any way you want, because God does not count even the good you do as anything. God is not interested in what percentage of the commandments you are keeping or not keeping. He is interested in you being the kind of person who desires to keep commandments, who loves to keep the commandments, and who keeps the commandments naturally, whether or not there is a reward for keeping them or a punishment for not keeping them. God is after your heart, the best of it. Doing your best to be good because of fear of the fire and fury of God does not make you a good person. Being good truly comes from the inside. Therefore, it is abundantly clear that one of the goals God seeks to achieve through the gospel of His grace is to show man who He is. The law was developed to show a sinner who they are - a cold, uncaring, rotten sinner. However, by removing the constraints of the law through the gospel, God then wants the saint to reveal who they are — a child of God who loves God from the heart and does all they do out of genuine love for God.

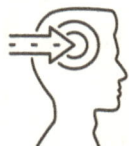

DEEPENING YOUR UNDERSTANDING

What does this all mean?

- What other examples can you recall where the Bible shows how the law is used as a tutor to bring men to Jesus the Savior? Why is it impossible to get people to truly believe the good news without their understanding of the bad news (humanity's fallen state before a perfect God)? Why is this use of the law not that common today? How could this account for questionable conversion that seems prevalent today? How would this change how we evangelize?

- Two people go into God's house to pray: one is praying under the law, and the other is praying under grace. How would you know the difference? Two people do not commit murder: one does not commit it under the law, and the other does not commit it under grace. How could you tell the difference? Two people do not commit fornication: one does not commit it under the law, and the other does not commit it under grace. How would you tell the difference?

- Does Jesus require everyone to give up all their wealth before they can be saved? How does the instruction Jesus gave to the rich young man apply to other areas of our lives? Where else do you observe Jesus helping people see the nature of their hearts in this way?

- How is the law of love higher than the law? How is it that only through the gospel could love be the only motivation for keeping the law? Can someone keeping the law out of fear of punishment or desire for reward ever keep it out of love?

- How should a New Testament Christian read or react to the blessings in the Bible for keeping the commands of God and the curses on the wicked for breaking the commands of God?

 ## APPLYING WHAT YOU HAVE LEARNED

Now, what should I do?

- In what ways can you use the law as a practical way of living your life without making it the basis of your acceptance with God?

- Make a list of blessings that belong to the righteous mentioned in the Old Testament. How can you develop the confidence to appropriate these blessings for yourself?

- Psalm 1:2 says, "But his delight is in the law of the LORD; and in his law does he meditate day and night" (King James 2000 Bible). How can you delight in the law of God when it is filled with commands you are either struggling to keep or breaking?

CHAPTER 9

Dismantling Your Idols

It is for freedom that Christ has set us free. Stand firm, then, and do not let yourselves be burdened again by a yoke of slavery. Mark my words! I, Paul, tell you that if you let yourselves be circumcised, Christ will be of no value to you at all. Again I declare to every man who lets himself be circumcised that he is obligated to obey the whole law. You who are trying to be justified by the law have been alienated from Christ; you have fallen away from grace. For through the Spirit we eagerly await by faith the righteousness for which we hope. For in Christ Jesus neither circumcision nor uncircumcision has any value. The only thing that counts is faith expressing itself through love (Galatians 5:1–6 NIV).

There is one particular sin that is the number one enemy of God in our lives. It is a sin that easily besets us, is beneath all other sins, and seeks to enslave us perpetually. This sin is the sin of idolatry - the making or keeping of idols in our lives and hearts. An idol is anything more important than God in your life; anything that absorbs your heart and imagination more than God; anything - good, bad, or ugly - the plays the role only God ought to play in your life. It is anything that you seek to obtain that only God can give to you. An idol is whatever you look at and say, deep within your heart of hearts, "If only I could have that, then I'll feel my life has meaning. Then, I'll know I have value; I'll feel significant and secure. If only I could have this, then I will feel happy, satisfied, and complete." In other words, you have come to see that thing as your "savior," the thing that would make you whole. It could be a person, a job, a fantasy, a feeling, an achievement. It could be anything.

Lots of words can be used to describe when we have that kind of relationship to something, but perhaps the best one is worship. This is why idolatry is the very first sin God warns us against in the very First Commandment: "I am the LORD your God…you shall have (worship) no other gods before me…" (Exodus 20:3). This is what Paul described in Romans 1:25 when he says

> "We never break the other commandments of God without first breaking the commandment against idolatry – the first commandment." – Martin Luther

people "…worship and serve the creature more than the Creator." Right after this statement, Paul makes a long list of sins, directly implying that all our failures to live right are rooted in this original, underlying sin of idolatry. When we make anything but God, our Savior, our ultimate source of happiness, we have set up an idol, have committed the sin of idolatry, and are on our way to be becoming idolaters. Remember this when next you read about the idol worshippers in the Old Testament.

Take the sin of anger, for example. You will only remain mad at someone if you believe that someone or some circumstance is getting in the way of something (other than God) that is key to your well-being and happiness. If God is your ultimate source of well-being, it is impossible to stay mad at anyone, because they are not God. Your acknowledging God as the source of your well-being means that ultimately you know that these people who may be getting in your way cannot affect your well-being. And so you are able to calm down and refuse to stay angry at them.

Another example is the sin of sexual lust and immorality. Sexual lust is nothing but a strong desire to consume the body of someone else because you feel that doing so is key to your happiness and achievement. You have come to believe that consuming someone else's body will save you from the unhappiness and loneliness you currently feel. Alas, this is a false god, an idol, as so many have found, to their great dismay. For after you have consumed tens and hundreds of beautiful or handsome human bodies, you are still left empty and wanting. Why? Because you tried to drive from sexual interaction that which can only be provided by God.

Look at the sin of greed. Greed is nothing but making wealth and its accumulation the ultimate source of your safety, joy, security, power, or happiness. When you have done this, you find yourself doing anything to accumulate it or not lose it including hoarding, lying, cheating, and worse. I could go on and on, but I am sure you get the point. Take any sin and trace it all the way down, and you will find that at its root is an idol - something or someone other than

God who has been made the source of your happiness and fulfillment in life, in short, your "savior." Note that none of these things are bad in themselves. Money is good. Companionship is good. Being liked and respected by people is good. Comfort is good. But when we make a good thing an ultimate thing, when we turn a good thing into a "god-thing," we commit idolatry and make the creation equal to the creator. Thus, they enslave us.

We see, then, that at the root of idolatry is a failure to actively continue in grace - in what God is to us and what He has done for us in Christ Jesus. When we forget the truth of what God has done for us, we slip back into looking for what other things can do for us. As long as we are resting on what God has done for us, it is impossible for our hearts to long for what other things can do for us. If we are satisfied with God, we will not need to seek satisfaction from someone or something else. This is how a Christian, by continuing in grace — growing deeper into what God has done and being rooted and established in it — goes on to live a life of holiness and purity. Continuing in grace deals with the root of the problem — the insatiable desire and search for salvation from other things.

How does knowing this, therefore, enable us to gain victory over "the sin that doth easily beset us" (Hebrews 12:1), so we can achieve our ultimate goal of becoming more like Jesus? When we sin, we are "forgetting" the truth of the gospel — who God is to us and what God has done for us in Christ. We are instead being moved by some idol. Hence, Paul admonishes us to "always remember what God has done for us in Christ and stand fast in the freedom we have as a result of what God has done!" (Galatians 5:1 paraphrased). Hold on to it; go deeper into it; be more grounded in it. How can we do this?

Let's say, for example, that you are struggling with sexual lust in your heart. Ask yourself what it is about the person(s) that is making you desire to consume them in this way? Pleasure? Acceptance? Companionship? Fun? Selfishness (i.e., wanting to be your savior)? Dismantle that idol by seeking those things not from a person but from what God has done for you already in Christ Jesus! Can you see that you are the bride of Christ? He loves you passionately and intimately, more than any woman or man could ever love you! Do you know that at this very moment, Jesus is with you as a lover, as a friend that is closer than a brother, and a brother who is there at all times? Can you see that He is not just with you but also in you—in a way deeper than you could ever be with or in anyone? If the gospel of what God has done for you is true, can you see that your hunger and need for intimacy, to know and be known, is fully met in God and by God through Jesus? As this happens — as God meets your deepest needs — all of a sudden, the need to consume another in your lust, or to use people to meet this need disappears. As you continue in grace, the foundations of idolatry in your life are dismantled. Slowly but surely, you begin to experience freedom from sins that have plagued you. This is how continuing in grace liberates you to be who you are in Christ.

If you are a workaholic, what is it that your heart has made an idol? Approval, respect, or admiration from people? Financial security? Power over people? Dismantle that idol by looking for approval, safety, and financial security from what God has done for you in Christ alone. Suddenly you will be free from the need to work so much. When you begin to see how much God approves of you, how He admires you for who you are and who He has made you. Of course you do not stop working. However, you will stop working for the wrong reasons. You do not stop working hard when you come to see how, because of what Jesus has done, God has already blessed you and that if God could give up Jesus for you, there is nothing He would withhold from you. However, your faith is no longer in your hard work, but in God, who is working through you.

Do you find yourself being too talkative? Are you a talebearer, a constant gossip, or a compulsive liar? Ask yourself: what is it that my heart has made an idol? Why am I behaving this way? Is it a need to be on the inside, to be among, not to be left out, or to be seen as the one with the latest information? Dismantle that idol by looking for these things not from gossip and talebearing but from what God has done for you in Christ alone. The truth of the gospel says that because of what Jesus did, you are now the ultimate insider; you are now a part of the Godhead. You are no longer on the periphery trying to get in. God has brought you in. You are an insider in the heavenly court of the Father and the Son and the Holy Spirit. You are now an insider with all the great saints of God. You are now a part of the commonwealth of Israel (Ephesians 2:12). Therefore, you do not need to be a talebearer, a gossip, or a carrier of information so that people can bring you inside. You are inside already. Suddenly, the need to talk and carry news disappears.

Dismantling Your Idols

Do you struggle with sharing your faith with others, praying for the sick, and ministering the gospel with boldness in public? Ask yourself: what is it that my heart has made an idol that is holding me back and making me act in this way? Is it fear of being rejected? Is it love of company? Whatever it is, dismantle that idol by looking for those things from what God did for you in Christ alone. Suddenly, you will be free to speak up for Jesus whenever and wherever you are.

> "Take me to you, O God, imprison me, for I,
> Except you enthrall me, never shall be free,
> Nor ever chaste, except you ravish me."
> -*Holy Sonnets by John Donne*

It was for your freedom from idols and false gods that Christ came to set you free! Because of who God is to you and what He has done for you in Christ, you do not need to make anything else your ultimate prize. Let Jesus set you free. Stand fast, therefore, in your freedom and hold on to it. Grip it firmly, grasp it with all your might, do not let it go, and be grounded in it. Go deeper and dig out anything that enslaves by pretending that it can give you what only God could ever give you, indeed, what God has already given you in Jesus! Dismantle your idols! Go all the way down to the deepest part of your souls, and deal with the cancer of sinful habits in your life at its very roots. Then you will experience true and lasting freedom and begin to manifest the reality of who you are in God—a son or daughter of the Most High.

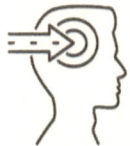# DEEPENING YOUR UNDERSTANDING

What does this mean?

- How does seeing sin in this way — an act that stems from something we have made an idol of — make us appreciate the evil of sin? Why would seeing sin this way make the young woman who sleeps with her married benefactor the same as the pastor who lied that he prayed for a church member when he forgot to do so? How does knowing what God has done for you in Jesus help the pastor have no need to lie, or the young woman to give in to her married benefactor's advances?

- In the Old Testament, God called idolatry adultery because it is, at its core, unfaithfulness and estrangement from God. In Galatians 5:4, Paul says we have "fallen from grace, estranged from Christ" if we seek to be justified (accepted by God) through our efforts to keep the law. How and why could someone who is assiduously obeying the commands of the law have an idol in their heart that this person is enslaved to? How can Christians seek to obey God's law and not be enslaved by idols?

- Author Lee C Turner, from his book Grace Discipleship Course, says: "Everybody is a slave. All we get to do is choose who to be a slave to." Do you think this sentiment is true? How does this choice to be a slave to God make us truly free? How does choosing to be a slave to other things ultimately lead to our destruction?

APPLYING WHAT YOU'VE LEARNED

Now, what do I do?

- In what specific area of your life will the truth of the gospel—the truth about what God has already done for you in Jesus—be able to deliver you from slavery to the idols of your heart? What can you do today to stand fast in your freedom and refuse to be entangled again in the yoke of slavery?

- Make a list of a few things you know are idols in your heart. Make a second list of truths of what God has done for you in Jesus that set you free from them. What can you do to set the whole of your heart on the things God has done to free you from the idols of your heart?

CHAPTER 10

Walk in the Spirit

I say then: Walk in the Spirit, and you shall not fulfill the lust of the flesh. For the flesh lusts against the Spirit, and the Spirit against the flesh; and these are contrary to one another so that you do not do the things that you wish. But if the Spirit leads you, you are not under the law. Now the works of the flesh are evident, which are: adultery, fornication, uncleanness, lewdness, idolatry, sorcery, hatred, contentions, jealousies, outbursts of wrath, selfish ambitions, dissensions, heresies, envy, murders, drunkenness, revelries, and the like; of which I tell you beforehand, just as I also told you in time past, that those who practice such things will not inherit the kingdom of God. But the fruit of the Spirit is love, joy, peace, longsuffering, kindness, goodness, faithfulness, gentleness, self-control. Against such there is no law. And those who are Christ's have crucified the flesh with its passions and desires. If we live in the Spirit, let us also walk in the Spirit (Galatians 5:16–25 NKJV).

Our natural selves (our human bodies and souls, i.e., our personalities) were always meant to yield as slaves to the true God, dwelling in our spirit-man. When humankind rebelled and was cut off from the true God, two things happened. First, we acquired evil, sinful natures (what Paul sometimes calls the "old man") from Adam, a dead spirit-man, who, disconnected from the life of God, lived in constant fear of God and rebelled against God. Secondly, with a dead spirit-man cut off from the true life that is in God, our natural selves (our human bodies and souls, i.e., our personalities) begin to act independently of God. Your natural self, operating independently of God, is what Paul calls "the flesh" (Greek: sarx, or "dead meat"). As dead meat attracts flies, your natural self, operating independently of the life of God (i.e., the flesh) has an intense proclivity to attract "spiritual flies." By that, I mean that in its craving for life, the flesh develops a proclivity to take good things and turn them into god-alternatives or "god-things." These good things turned to "god-things" are what are known as idols of the heart.

A sinner who has not yet received the life of Jesus has a powerful one-two combination, making it impossible for him to live the life God desires for him. First, he is a dead spirit-man who constantly wants to live in rebellion against God. Second, this sinful nature, or old man, is then constantly providing to our flesh (our natural self, operating independently of the life of God) with a host of idols or enemies of God to worship. When we, therefore, say that we are saved by "the grace of God" or "the works of God in our lives in Jesus Christ," we mean that the sinful nature, or old man, where sin (or rebellion against God) dwelt, has been crucified with Christ. In exchange, we received a divine nature, a living spirit-man, a new man—created after Jesus and the Spirit of God, perfected for every good work. This is where, for the most part, the work of God's grace has been done in our lives.

Therefore, as a Christian, I have two choices. On the one

hand, I could choose to still live in the natural self, operating independently of God (which was my habit before I was saved). I would do this by allowing my natural senses, my natural personality, and my natural mind to choose and make decisions on how I feel about myself. I could choose to base my acceptance with God, my happiness, and my self-esteem on things that I have, things that I see, or perceive in the natural world. Whenever I make this choice, Paul says, I am "living in the flesh," I am "carnally minded," I am "walking in the flesh," and I am "putting on the old man." When I live in the flesh, I will fulfill the "lusts" (Greek: epithumia, or "to over-desire something") of the flesh. This means that whenever I choose to live in this way, I will give my natural self a chance to operate independently of the life of God and thus take anything—even good things—and turn them into ultimate things: god-alternatives or idols.

This happens not because there is anything inherently bad with my natural self, but simply because my natural self needs life outside itself to live. In other words, it needs a god to worship, a god to give it life, and a god to be a slave to. That is the way it was made. As a result, if I live in the flesh, what will manifest in my life will be the "works of the flesh" things I will be doing to worship, protect, promote, and preserve these good things that I have turned into ultimate things: sexual immorality, uncleanness, lasciviousness, idolatry, witchcraft, hatred, variance, emulations, wrath, strife, seditions, heresies, feelings of envy, murders, drunkenness, revelry, and such. Paul makes it clear that if we lived in this way, we would exclude ourselves from the enjoyment of the kingdom of God and all that it provides.

Think about this! Paul is saying here that if someone is focused on how well they are keeping the law, as one example of operating in the flesh, what they will experience is not a righteous life but a sinful life. Living under the law will not produce obedience to the law; rather, it will produce greater and greater disobedience to the law! Why? Because that was NEVER how we were meant to live! We were never meant to live by observing in the natural what good things we were doing or what bad things we were doing (which is what the law does). We were meant to live by observing in the Spirit what our Father God has done and is doing and living from what God has done and is doing, not what we do. Through Moses, God put the law in place to show us how sinful we become when we do try to live our lives without God.

> The "Works of the flesh" are the things that I will end up doing if my goal is to protect, promote and preserve the good things of life that I have turned into ultimate things.

So how and why does this happen? How can I, by focusing on how well I am keeping the law, become a breaker of the same law? The answer is found in what the Bible calls "the weakness of the flesh" (Romans 8:3). The flesh, having no life in itself (John 6:63), will always turn anything, in this case, a good thing like a sincere, earnest effort to keep the law, into a "god-thing." It will always look for life outside itself. The fact, however, is that as good as the law of God is, it has no life in it. Life is in God—not in God's laws. The law, while telling you what to do or not to do, does not have the power to help you do it. Focusing on the law to produce righteousness in you is like trying to use a looking glass to cleanse your face! What ends up happening is this: rather than focusing on keeping the law to arouse faith in God, it arouses all kinds of god-alternatives—or as Paul puts it, "sinful passions" or "evil desires."

Take, for example, someone who draws life from the fact that he does not commit adultery, commit sexual sin, or covet someone else's wife. This man will wake up every day making all sorts of arrangements, rules, and regulations to maintain this commitment to adultery-free or covetousness-free living, believing that success in this area is life and the basis of his acceptance with God. However, what all of these will stir up is stronger and stronger passions and desires within him, eventually driving him to get involved in the very adultery and sexual sins he is trying to avoid. Not desiring someone who is not his wife would be a constant internal battle he would be fighting. Because there is no life in the law "thou shalt not commit adultery," his natural self, independent of the life of God (i.e., his flesh) is powerless against the overwhelming desire to commit this sin. With each passing day, all the focus on this law simply stirs up stronger and stronger desires in his flesh to do the very thing he does not want to do! The evil desires within him become stronger and stronger until—inevitably and invariably—one day he will cross whatever lines he set for himself as he inches closer and closer toward adultery.

To deal with this, the man, at best, is forced to come up

with new rules to excuse why the ones he had set before failed and why he was unable to meet them. At worst, as is often the case, he begins to excuse and justify himself or begins to categorize the different levels of the sin or play other mental gymnastics, all in an attempt to avoid the inevitable conclusion that if life comes by keeping this law, he has cut himself off from life by breaking it multiple times. Often, such a person becomes a hypocrite, openly criticizing the same sin he practices in secret. This is the reason why, when you walk into a legalistic church community, you will find a preponderance of simultaneously contradicting rules required for "holy living." At the same time, a preponderance of secret sins exists among the members of that community. Any attempt to receive life from how well people are keeping the law is "walking in the flesh." Also, walking in the flesh will produce the works of the flesh listed in Galatians 5, because all flesh will do is to turn that attempt to keep the law into an idol.

On the other hand, as a Christian, I could instead choose to allow all that God has done for me in the Spirit to dictate to me how I will behave. Paul says living this way is "living in the Spirit," "walking in the Spirit," "being led by the Spirit," or "putting on the new man." Jesus calls it "living in me," "following me," or "abiding in me." If I live in this way, I will not be under the law (Galatians 5:18), i.e., who I am or what I receive will not be determined by how well I keep the law. I will no longer feel the need to keep the law to be accepted by God. Before I was saved, living by the Spirit was unavailable to me; furthermore, the old man made sure I was rebellious toward God and continued to choose other gods. Further, by living in the Spirit, I will be working out the crucifixion of the old man and the flesh, which has already happened in Jesus (Galatians 5:24, Romans 6:6). The ability of my natural self to dictate what I should worship or lust after continues to diminish. I will no longer be a factory of idols, someone who is constantly turning good things into ultimate things, which, as we have already seen, is the root of all sin. Even more, I will begin to produce the fruit of the Spirit—a lifestyle filled with all the good things God has done in me—love, joy, peace, longsuffering, gentleness, goodness, faith, meekness, temperance, and so on. Paul says that with this fruit flowing naturally out of my life, I will keep the entire law without even trying.

How does this happen? How can I, by focusing on what God has already done for me in Christ Jesus, experience life and progressively overcome sin while manifesting the fruit of the Spirit? The answer lies in

> The "Fruit of the Spirit" is what manifests in my life when I am, through the help of God's Spirit, focused on practicing, promoting and praising God for what God has already done for me and in me in Christ Jesus.

the fact that "while the flesh profits nothing, the Spirit is what gives life" (John 6:63). Living by the Spirit is a walk of faith. It is living from the inside out. It starts from a place that says: "God already loves me. God already accepts me.

It is not because of what I do, but because of what Jesus has done." You are therefore drawing life from God Himself—from who He is and what He has done! Nothing comes from yourself or anything else outside you. Life alone is found in God, and it must be from Him alone that we must seek it.

Take, for example, someone who draws life from God in this way. They wake up every morning rejoicing and thankful to God that they do not have to do anything that day to earn God's love or acceptance. They are already fully accepted! He is fully loved! Just that realization alone fills their hearts with so much warmth and love and gratitude. As the man or woman step out into the day, they will sense their flesh trying to find life in other things—in sexual feelings, in money, in acceptance of people, and in fame and popularity. They sense these "evil desires" or lusts of the flesh trying to creep up on them, but they know deep within themselves that they already have life from God! They do not need anything or anyone to give them life. The most beautiful eyes in the universe already accept them. The One whose opinion matters already said to them: "You are okay. I love you." So what do they do? They double down on the life they are getting from full acceptance from God! They dig in deeper into that life! They plug their natural selves back into the life of God by exclaiming: "Bless the Lord, O my soul; And all that is within me, bless His holy name! Bless the Lord, O my soul, And forget not all His benefits: Who forgives all your iniquities, Who heals all your diseases, Who redeems your life from destruction, Who crowns you with lovingkindness and tender mercies, Who satisfies your mouth with good things, So that your youth is renewed like the eagle's" (Psalm 103:1–5).

They engage in a fight of faith to bring their whole selves to see, by faith, all that God has already done for them. By doing so, their affections and desires begin to change back to that which is of God. In doing so, they progressively starve their flesh of all its effort to look for life in other things! They live in the Spirit (i.e., in that which God has done for him in Jesus) so that they do not fulfill the lust of the flesh (the natural self, acting independently of the life of God).

We see then the secret of holy living according to the gospel of God's grace: it is not to try harder to avoid sin but to try harder to rest in God and draw life from God Himself. It is holy living by displacement — by simply focusing more and more on the life God has given you. Therefore, death diminishes in your life more and more. It means to dig deeper into how well you have been loved by God. It is not to work the law harder but to rest harder on God, in His love for you, and on what He has done for you. As your affections are overwhelmed by this incredible experience, the taste for all that is sin begins to disappear in your life. Here is how Paul puts it in Ephesians 3:14-19: "For this reason I bow my knees to the Father of our Lord Jesus Christ, from whom the whole family in heaven and earth is named, that He would grant you, according to the riches of His glory, to be strengthened with might through His Spirit in the inner man, that Christ may dwell in your hearts through faith; that you, may be rooted and grounded in His love, having to comprehended and known the width and length and depth and height of the love of Christ which passes knowledge; this way, you will be filled with all the fullness of God."

Here is the truth of the gospel, if you have received the life of God in Christ: you no longer have a sinful nature! That nature was crucified with Christ. You died to sin when Jesus died. Jesus, through His death, killed that rebel in you and in its place is a new person—a person created in the righteousness of God. A person filled with the life and love of God. A person that, if allowed, will always produce fruits of love, goodness, kindness, gentleness, and so on, in you. It is a God-possessed inner person. It is the real you. However, you are still carrying about a soul and a body that for years learned to live as slaves to the old man—the man of sin. Our goal as Christians is to "walk in the Spirit," i.e., retrain our natural man to no longer live as slaves to the old man who is now dead and gone, but to be the new man, who is our real selves. This is what Paul means when he says, "work out the salvation that you have experienced in Jesus, for God has already worked it in you." Therefore, to walk in the Spirit is not a mystical thing. It is simply an intentional, daily decision not to do what the old man had trained you to do but to live out instead what you know you have become in the Spirit. This is why we must make an effort daily to discover the things of this new man. This is also why we attend church services, enjoy fellowship with other believers regularly, read the Bible, and pray together. Through these activities, we continue to discover who we are so we can decide to live it out.

In 2015, I read the book *Letters of a Mystic* by Frank Laubach. It is the diary of a man who decided never to allow one minute to pass by without him turning his mind completely over to God. I decided to try this myself—to make a conscious effort to turn my thoughts and mind over to God at least once every minute of the day. This meant either thinking upon a verse scripture, deliberately thinking of or talking to the Holy Spirit about everything that came to my mind, or just actively singing and worshipping God while meditating on the song. As you can imagine, this was a real struggle. I found that my natural mind and natural senses vehemently resisted surrendering control to God's Spirit. They had been independent for so long—it was a war to quell their uprising, so I barely succeeded in my goal for more than 20 percent of the time. Nevertheless, for that 20 percent, the results were magnificently astounding. For the first time in my life, I felt fully alive as I felt the power of my mind become unleashed in an unprecedented way. I finally understood what Jesus meant by "apart from Me, you can do nothing" (John 15:5) or that "the Son does nothing except what he sees the Father do" (5:19). I also understood how an ordinary carpenter (Jesus) could know law, theology, astronomy, agronomy, fishery, meteorology, medicine, and government. No, it was not because he was God. Rather, as a man, Jesus yielded his entire mind, the source of human action, to the Spirit of God. During that time, all I needed to do was simply to think of something, and it would happen—because the One thinking through me was the Spirit of God Himself. I would know things without learning them! My eyes could see things and perceive things about people and situations. I could do a far better job with my clients, and I spoke to them with unprecedented wisdom. My mind became a tool in the hand of the Almighty to do great things. I became truly "spiritually minded" and "lived in the Spirit." I discovered that God never made our minds and senses to be independent of Him—they operate at their fullest potential when God directs them. Like fish in the oceans, our minds operate at their optimum when living in the ocean of the Divine.

I was so overwhelmed by what was happening to me that I cried to God to stop it—and He did. I was not ready to live at that level then and could not handle the experience. But I feel like I am now. I invite you to join me as Paul said, "If we have received life in the Spirit, let us walk in the Spirit" — moment by moment, minute by minute (Galatians 5:25). Let's see if we can live on this earth as sons and daughters of God.

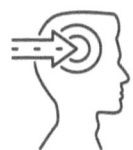

DEEPENING YOUR UNDERSTANDING

What does this mean?

- Paul suggests that when we attempt to find acceptance with God through the law or good efforts, we are walking in the flesh. If this is true, list some works of the flesh that would be observed in a person who is seeking to be justified by their efforts to keep the law.

- We often define lust simply as sexual sin, but lust means to over-desire, to make a good thing into an ultimate thing. How and why is the New Testament "lust" similar to or the same thing as Old Testament "idolatry"? How does this insight help us understand why the Israelites kept falling into the sin of idolatry, or why the New Testament calls "fleshly lusts" the enemy of God in our lives?

- Does a born-again Christian have one nature or two natures? Is he or she a saint, a sinner, or a sinner-saint combo?

- What is the difference between the "flesh" (i.e., your natural self and personality) and the "sinful nature" or "old man" (the part of you that was in rebellion against God)? When the Bible says that Jesus Christ came in the flesh, does this mean that He had a sinful nature? How does understanding this difference help clarify if a born-again Christian has one or two natures?

 APPLYING WHAT YOU HAVE LEARNED

Now, what do I do?

- How can you pray and meditate so that you can constantly keep the Lord in your mind for a significant portion of the day? Construct a prayer that would help you constantly direct and redirect your mind to the Lord and Holy Spirit frequently.

- How can you keep yourself from idols (1 John 5:21)? What idols resonate most with you? In what ways can you free yourself from idols by living in the Spirit rather than in your flesh or natural self?

CHAPTER 11

From Nothing to Something

For if anyone thinks himself to be something, when he is nothing, he deceives himself. But let each one examine his work, and then he will have rejoicing in himself alone, and not in another. For each one shall bear his own load (Galatians 6:3–5).

Having dealt with how living according to the truth of the gospel affects our individual lives (i.e., freedom to live in the Spirit), Paul turned his attention to how the truth of the gospel impacts how we live in the community. Remember that the gospel is the good news of what God has done for an undeserving man in Christ. In other words, we who are NOTHING have been made SOMETHING by God in Christ Jesus. This is why Paul says in Galatians 6:3 that a man who thinks he is SOMETHING when he is NOTHING deceives himself and is not living according to the truth of the gospel. He affirms that as long as we hold on to the truth of the gospel that we are NOTHING whom God made SOMETHING, it will have an impact on 1) how we relate with one another; 2) how we relate with people in our midst who are overtaken by sin; and 3) how we support one another, especially those who are most vulnerable, in our midst.

First, let's see how it impacts how we relate to one another. In Galatians 5:26, Paul says if we believed the truth of the gospel, i.e., that we are NOTHING whom God made SOMETHING in Christ, we will not be "conceited" or "vainglorious" or as the Message Bible translation puts it, we will not "compare ourselves with each other as if one of us were better and another worse" (MSG) The Greek word used here is *kenodoxos*. It means "empty glory"— what a person does to prop himself up and try to appear as if he is SOMETHING, when, in his heart of hearts, he knows deep within himself that he is NOTHING, and he has NO GLORY (Romans 3:23). If we ever believe or act as if anything in the natural such as money, knowledge, beauty, education, size of business, size of church, profession, number of children, marital status, political status, and so on, and yes, even keeping of God's laws, is the reason why we are SOMETHING, we will invariably become conceited or vainglorious.

> We who are NOTHING have been made SOMETHING by God in Christ Jesus.

Have you ever wondered why it seems as though Christians can't get along? You may find a community of believers that, based on what they teach and profess, you expect it to be a stronghold of love and peace and harmony. Instead, what you notice are born-again, tongue-talking, Holy-Ghost filled, demon-casting-out believers who cannot seem to stand each other. Like the Prophet Isaiah said of God in Isaiah 5:7, "..*the vineyard of the LORD Almighty is the nation of Israel, and the people of Judah are the vines he delighted in, and he looked for justice but saw bloodshed; for righteousness, but heard cries of distress....*" I strongly believe that what Paul was describing in Galatians 5:26 is the mindset and the reason why the vineyard of the Lord, the church, the body of Christ, could be a place that produces bloodshed instead of justice and cries of distress instead of righteousness. According to Paul, the two fundamental enemies of all human relationships are a superiority complex (when those of us who have these things think we are SOMETHING because of the things we have and thus "provoke" or "challenge" or "insult" others) and an inferiority complex (when those of us who do not have these things envy or are unable to relate with those who have them, because we think we are nothing because we do not have them).

Let's dive into this a little. In Galatians 5:26, Paul states that "vainglory" or "comparing ourselves with each other as if one of us were better and another worse" would cause one of two things to happen. First, either we "provoke one another" or we "envy one another." In my view, both of these phrases summarize all the things that lead to the deterioration of human relationships. Take the phrase "provoking one another." The word used in the original Greek, *prokaleo*, means to irritate someone by constantly announcing, calling forth, or acting as if you are in front of them or ahead of them. It means to dare them or challenge them to catch up with you. In Nigeria, where I was born, it is called "to oppress" another with your show of wealth, fame, connections, beauty, or whatever. We can see why living in the flesh— including measuring yourself with how well you are keeping the law—will produce this sense of superiority in someone and consequently lead to the destruction of relationships. Without the truth of the gospel, which makes us understand that we are all NOTHING whom God made SOMETHING in Jesus, the moment we come into a relationship with someone else, we would immediately begin to assess whether this person is at our level, or we begin to flaunt our fleshly accomplishment to establish the fact that we are not at their level. This is what leads us to put people down, condescend to them, behave smugly, be snobbish, or exhibit false humility. So we end up provoking the other person. We need the truth of the gospel that no one is ANYTHING—except what God has made him or her in Jesus.

The second phrase Paul used was "envying one another." The original language connotes looking up at someone and being mad about their status in life. It means to have an ill will toward people because you are upset about what they may or may not have achieved and because they appear better, smarter, or more beautiful than you. They have or are receiving something you believe you should have rather than them, and it makes you very upset. This happens whenever someone who thinks he is NOTHING because he does not have SOMETHING another person has, or when people think they have SOMETHING another person has, but they do not. Envy is what happens when your nothingness meets the nothingness of another who yet appears better than you or is getting a better deal than you, and you wonder why. This, then, leads to self-talk that goes something like this: "Oh, take a look at this person who is nothing, just like I am nothing and yet they are so rich, so nice, so smart, so talented, so beautiful, and seem to have everything." Before you know it, you resent the unfairness of it all, you begin to spend time pointing out the nothingness of the person in an attempt to feel better about yourself, or you begin to attack any good thing said about them. This is where you need the truth of the gospel to deliver you—the truth that says even though you are nothing, you are something because of what Jesus did, and the other person who seems to have things actually has nothing over you because if they are anything, it is also because of being something because of Jesus.

Continuing to deal with the impact of the gospel in the community, Paul shows how we would deal with each other when we are overtaken by sin if we truly believed the truth of the gospel that we are NOTHING whom God has made SOMETHING. We see this in Galatians 6:1-3. Let me paraphrase those verses: "If a brother is living on the outside the way he is not on the inside (a fault overtakes him), those of us who know what it means to live on the outside the way we are on the inside (who are spiritual) should help this person to become on the outside who he is on the inside (restore him or help him find his true self)—but do this in all gentleness—not in a harsh or judgmental way, but as gently as a mother treats her child and a father his children (1 Thessalonians 2:7-12)—considering yourself and remembering that, but for what God had done for you, you yourself are NOTHING—lest you be tempted—to think yourself as SOMETHING—and then become prideful and conceited. For if a man thinks himself to be something when he is nothing, he deceives himself!" Can we see how different those verses now read and how powerfully they communicate the love of God in Jesus? These verses present to us the perspective, the person, the purpose, and the process necessary for appropriate intervention as a gospel community when we come upon a brother or sister overtaken by sin.

First is the perspective necessary for appropriate intervention. Note the phrase Paul used to describe the situation. He speaks of someone overtaken by a fault. To be overtaken means "to catch up with and pass, to come suddenly upon." In other words, this was unexpected. This is not normal. Something that was supposed to happen has been overtaken by something that was not supposed to happen. The thing that this person did is not who the person is. By implication, it means that for us to intervene appropriately, we must believe that this is someone living on the outside in a way that is not consistent with who they are. In other words, Paul wants us to look beyond the outward actions of this person, to refuse to identify this person with what they did, to in effect choose to "walk in the Spirit" when it comes to how we see each other when we sin. We must be able to say to ourselves and the person overtaken by fault: "My brother, my sister, I know this is not who you are." We must see the brother or sister as having been overtaken, taken captive in this situation.

Paul says having this view gives us the appropriate perspective to appropriately intervene. Until you can see your brother or sister as having been "overtaken by a fault," Paul strongly advises that you do not make any attempt to mount an intervention. We see Paul himself adopting this perspective when he addressed the hypocrisy of Peter when the Jews came from Jerusalem and Peter withdrew from fellowshipping with the

Gentiles. Paul confronted Peter from the perspective of "You are not walking in line with who you are, Peter." Hence, he says, "when I saw that they did not walk in line with the truth of the gospel." He did not call Peter a hypocrite; rather, he said he did not walk in line with who he was. Holding this perspective is foundational to handling conflict and intervening when a fault overtakes a brother or sister.

The next point we see here is the person necessary for appropriate intervention. Paul says those who are "spiritual." If we keep faith with the definitions we have used in this book, it should be clear to us who Paul has in mind here and what Paul means when he uses the word "spiritual." Paul is not looking for someone who is sitting on a holier-than-thou seat. He does not mean someone who has never been taken by a fault. He is not talking about someone who is spooky or weird or acting abnormally. To be "spiritual" simply means that you are practicing to be on the outside who you are on the inside. It means that you see yourself as a bundle of love, goodness, kindness, faithfulness, and gentleness — and so you are constantly practicing to work these things out in your life. To be spiritual means that you are holding on to the "truth of the gospel" about yourself, even though you are observing so many things in the natural world seeming to suggest otherwise.

> To be "spiritual" simply means that you are practicing being on the outside who you are ALREADY on the inside.

If we understand this, we can see why it is an absolute imperative that only someone who is "spiritual" should get involved in an attempt to restore someone who is overtaken by a fault. This is so because it is ONLY someone who is working hard to be spiritual (i.e., is practicing living on the outside who they really are on the inside) — only such a person would clearly know what it means on an experiential level to be overtaken by a fault (i.e., to do something on the outside completely contrary to who you really are on the inside). Paul is, therefore, saying that if you have no personal, concrete experience in your own life of how you have been working out your salvation — with mistakes and all — then you are not the right person for this intervention. To be spiritual means that you are in a position to walk in love with the one who is overtaken by a fault. You have been where they are, too. This is why Paul says such a person must intervene, remembering and recognizing that he or she was NOTHING whom God made SOMETHING — lest they are tempted to think they are superior in any way!

We must also note the purpose of the intervention. Paul says the purpose of intervention is not to punish or discipline. The purpose of intervention is restoration. The first and most important purpose of the gospel community intervening when a fault overtakes someone is not to protect the community but to restore the person. It is to help the person get back to the place where they begin to work out and live on the outside what they are on the inside. Our goal as a gospel community must be to help the person see who they are in Christ — the SOMETHING God has made out of their NOTHING — and, seeing this, to "REPENT" by turning from this fault that has overtaken them and to begin to practice who they are. Only—and only if this person is unwilling to receive this loving intervention; if they remain stubborn and refuses to "repent," i.e., change their mind from thinking of themselves the wrong way, can a gospel community consider protecting itself from such a person. But protecting the community cannot be the original purpose of the spiritual intervention.

We must note the process of the intervention. It is done with gentleness, with patience, with an attitude of grace. Judgment must be set aside. Support systems must be created to help this person become fully restored to their place in their Father's house. We must do this knowing that we are NOTHING in ourselves and that God has made this person into SOMETHING—despite the fault, they have been overtaken. Paul also suggests that if we truly believe the truth of the gospel, we would see this ministry of restoration as one way through which, as brethren, we help bear one another's burdens and serve one another in love. In other words, only someone who has not truly examined himself (Galatians 6:4) and thinks he is SOMETHING when he is NOTHING will refuse such an important ministry from a fellow brother (6:2). Has a fault overtaken you? Do not hide in darkness! Allow the gospel community, through having the right perspective, person, purpose, and process of intervention, help you work your way back to living like who you are in Christ.

Finally, let me conclude this chapter by sharing how the truth of the gospel, that we are NOTHING whom God has made SOMETHING, helps a gospel community as it seeks to relate with the weak, vulnerable, and have-nots in our midst. Paul, in Galatians 6:6-10, suggests that if we believed the truth of the gospel that we are NOTHING whom God has made SOMETHING, we would be eager for God to use us to make others who may be NOTHING or have NOTHING to become SOMETHING—or have EVERYTHING. We will be eager to share the good things God has given us with others, especially with those spiritual leaders, pastors, and ministers whom God has used to announce to us what God has done for us in Christ. We will be eager to do good for others, especially those who are of the household of faith, no matter who they are or what they may or may not have, because we remember that we were NOTHING and had NOTHING when God stepped down to help us and make us SOMETHING. You see, how you treat or relate with someone who has nothing is driven more by how you see yourself than how you see the person. No one who genuinely sees himself as having become SOMETHING from NOTHING, purely by the grace of God—will ever look down on another person who has nothing. It is impossible! Anyone who looks down or criticizes or is condescending to someone who has nothing does so because they have never understood or never believed that he is NOTHING who was made something simply by grace.

This was powerfully represented and happened in the gospel community of the early church in Jerusalem. In Acts 4:33, we read that God's grace was powerfully at work in the midst of this gospel community. With one mind and one heart, they recognized that all of them—every single one of them was a NOTHING who had become SOMETHING because of the finished work of Jesus. As a result, not one of them claimed that anything belonged to them. Not one! How could they? Everyone recognized that they were NOTHING who became SOMETHING because of what God had done. How could they ever claim that they owned or merited anything? Consequently, they never allowed anyone to lack. The "rich" in their midst never allowed anyone who was poor and had nothing to remain that way; they knew that they were NOTHING when Jesus made them SOMETHING. The poor in their midst did not demand anything as a right from the rich. Neither also did they use the largesse of the rich as an opportunity to take more than what they needed. Why? Because they knew that even though they were NOTHING, Jesus had made them SOMETHING. They did not need to demand anything or take more than they needed from anyone to become SOMETHING. As Acts 4:34 states, "there were no needy...." Alleluia! In a gospel community, there is no one NEEDY. The rich did not need to hold on to their wealth, and the poor did not need the wealth of the rich. That is what happens when we all recognize that we who were nothing have become something—only because of what God has done for us in Jesus!

 DEEPENING YOUR UNDERSTANDING

What does this mean?
- Most of what is wrong with human relationships can be boiled down to either a superiority complex (provoking one another) or an inferiority complex (en-

vying one another). What do you think of this statement? How can these attitudes affect how we relate with each other in church? How does this affect the flow of love between brethren? Why are vainglory, conceit, or comparing ourselves with each other as if one of us were better and another worse the roots of problems between people?

- Outside the gospel, we are either confident or proud (if we are achieving) or humble (if we are failing). But in the gospel, our new self-image produces a bold humility that changes all relationships. What do you think about this statement? How does the truth of the gospel give you a bold humility and a new self-image?

- Paul encourages us to do a thorough examination of our work and ourselves, rather than to compare ourselves with others. Why? How can we perform this activity? What would a thorough and genuine self-examination produce in a person? How does doing this and having a correct view of ourselves (Galatians 6:3-5) influence how we treat others (Galatians 5:26 – 6:2)?

# APPLYING WHAT YOU HAVE LEARNED

Now, what do I do?

- KenoDoxos (conceit, vainglory) is the hunger to be important, the hunger to be something, the desire for glory that results from knowing deep within that you are nothing. All of us have sinned and have fallen short of God's glory. How does this manifest in your life? What can you do to deal with this? How do you currently handle this?

- Make a list of the reasons that Christians do so poorly at both Galatians 6:1-2 relationships. How well do you think your particular small group or church community is at the restoration stage of Galatians 6:1? What practical things could you do to do better at Galatians 6:2 and 6:1?

- You are a department head. A popular employee you hired is doing poorly and pulling the department's performance down. This employee richly deserves to be fired. What are some wrong ways to handle it, and what are some right ways?

- How can this approach help race relations, tribal relations, and gender relations in the church? How can it help you relate better with people who are different from you in status, race, class, gender, or tribe?

CHAPTER 12

Sustaining the Life of Grace

> *As many as desire to make a good showing in the flesh, these would compel you to be circumcised, only that they may not suffer persecution for the cross of Christ. For not even those who are circumcised keep the law, but they desire to have you circumcised that they may boast in your flesh. But God forbid that I should boast except in the cross of our Lord Jesus Christ, by whom the world has been crucified to me, and I to the world. For in Christ Jesus neither circumcision nor uncircumcision avails anything, but a new creation. And as many as walk according to this rule, peace and mercy be upon them, and upon the Israel of God. From now on let no one trouble me, for I bear in my body the marks of the Lord Jesus. Brethren, the grace of our Lord Jesus Christ be with your spirit. Amen (Galatians 6:12–18 NKJV).*

As Paul concludes his Letter to the Galatians, he gives three keys to sustaining the life of grace that we have received from God as a result of the work that God has begun in the Spirit in our lives, our churches, and our generation. To sustain the life and grow in the life of grace, we must recognize that the way we live our lives matters, the motives of our lives matters, and the mindsets we use to live our lives also matters.

First, he warns us never to be deceived and always to remember that the way we live our lives matters. Our actions have consequences! The way we live your life matters because we are either blessed or hurt not for what we do, but by what we do. We cannot live and operate in the natural world and not be hurt; neither can we live by the Spirit and not be blessed. Operating in the natural will produce idolatry — the root of all sin. Paul says, if we live this way — sowing to the natural — we will surely reap destruction. It could be in just one area — circumcision, the day of worship, dressing, praying methods, sexual relations, marriage, and yes, even in the keeping of the law. Once we operate in the natural in one area, sooner or later, death and destruction will spread, and the work of God in our lives will shut down. If we live in the Spirit — if we focus on who we are and what God has done in us, and as a result of that, commit to living out the good things that God has already deposited in us — it may be delayed, it may be slow, it may take time, but we will surely reap life.

> Be not deceived: the way we live our lives matter. Our actions have consequences.

Friend, do not ever think that you can mix flesh and Spirit and get away with it. No, you cannot! You cannot choose one day to live based on what you see in the natural and tomorrow, choose to live based on what is true in the Spirit. Whenever you live in the natural, you will unleash poisonous toxins into your life that will lead to death if not reversed. This is not God punishing you. This is you hurting yourself with bad choices. Paul uses the analogy of sowing and reaping to bring out this point: just as you do not see overnight the impact of a seed sown, so also you may not see overnight the impact of living in the flesh. But as surely as a seed was sown will sprout with fruits, so would living in the flesh produce death. This is a somber thought, and it is no wonder that you see churches and acts of God started in the Spirit, by faith in what God has done, yet over time, more and more is done or attempted through how well people keep laws and regulations. Slowly but surely, death creeps in, within a matter of time, that which was once a mighty move of God becomes nothing but a monument of devils. We must be very watchful: how we live matters! We must NEVER allow our lives to be based on what we do or see on the outside, such as how well we keep the laws, how big our congregations are, how big our temples are, how rich we are, and so on. If we sow in the flesh, if we live by what we observe in the natural, we will surely reap death. In the same way, if we sow in the Spirit, even if we do not see immediately the impact of our decision to only live by who we are in the Spirit, though it may tarry, the fruit of life will surely sprout. How you live your life today matters. Will you live by what you see in the natural, or will you go beyond the natural to live by who and what you are in the Spirit? Every day you must wake up and make up your mind to always sow in your Spirit. That which was begun in the Spirit can only be sustained in the Spirit. Do not fall back to the law, i.e., living in the flesh, to try to sustain what God began in the Spirit. Sow in the Spirit — every day, and as time passes, you will begin to see life sprout in every area of your life.

The second key to sustaining the work of God in our lives is to focus on our motives and to ensure that LOVE alone is the motive for ALL our actions. The way to accomplish this, Paul insists, is never to take any action or make people take any action if the reason for the action is NOT rooted in what God has ALREADY done for us in the finished work of Jesus on the cross (Galatians 6:14). We boast in the cross when we say something like "ONLY because of what God did for me on the cross, am I taking this action" and because what God did is a finished historical work, our action is, therefore, a love response to what Jesus has done already. This is how we can truly fulfill the 1 Corinthians 13:1-4 injunctions to make love the motive for all our actions, but if we say something like "it was because I did this and this, that God did that for me," then the motive for the action CAN NEVER be love. We have made the receipt of whatever it was that we wanted God to do for us the motive for our actions. Our boast is then in what we did or do for God to do something for us. That is what the Bible calls "dead works" or "works of the flesh." When we do "dead works," love, the key to God-life, is kicked out of our lives when we live in this way. Love as the only motive for our actions becomes our lifestyle as the gospel of grace opens our eyes to the many ways God acts in love toward us.

As we believe this, we too are able to act in love toward

> Do everything in love - *1 Corinthians 16:14 (NIV)*

others. It is impossible for a person to act in love toward another unless and until they first recognize that God has ALREADY acted toward us in LOVE. We love because He first loved us. God is already patient with us—so we can be patient with others as He has been with us. God is kind to us, and so we can be kind to others as He has been to us. God has not kept a record of our wrongs, and so we too can choose not to keep a record of wrongs against us. Without grace, without a commitment to living by grace, it is IMPOSSIBLE for love to be our only motive for living—and this motive is CRITICAL to sustaining the life of grace.

Finally, Paul reminds us that to keep the fire of God burning in our hearts and lives, we must never forget that, in Christ Jesus, although we are not what we do, we do get the chance to be who we are (Galatians 6:5). In other words, the focus here is not on what we do but on who we are. God is not focused on the number of good works you do as much as He is interested in the source of the good you do. If we focus on what we do—and teach that what we do is who we are, we are putting the cart before the horse. We will get involved in "behavior modification" and not heart change. We will make rules and laws to try to get people to conform to the image of who we want them to be. We will judge people by their actions. Thus, we are unable to perceive when God is still working on someone, even though it has not yet fully manifested on the outside. At the same time, we will not be able to perceive when God is not at work in someone's life, because they would be conforming to all the rules on the outside.

Nevertheless, if we teach people who they are in Jesus

and spend time, effort, and resources to patiently "present (show) every man how they are perfect (complete) in Christ" (Colossians 1:28), we can then admonish them to live out who they are in Christ. We can say to them and ourselves: "knowing that this is who you are, live in this way. Work out that which you are on the inside. Yes, you are not what you do. But who you are should be reflected in what you do." This way, we are in constant pursuit of godliness—the manifestation of the totality of our new nature in the natural. And so, even when we slip during our pursuit of godliness and act in ways that are not in line with who we are, we can pick ourselves up and continue to work toward restoration, recovery, and revival. This way, we will sustain the work of God and His work in the lives of people.

DEEPENING YOUR UNDERSTANDING

What does this mean?

- Actions have consequences; so, the way we live our lives matters. How does sowing to the flesh (e.g., living under the law) produce death? How does sowing in the spirit (living out who you are in Christ) produce life?

- Why is it possible for love to be the only motive for our actions if we boast in the cross? Why is it impossible if our boast is in keeping the law? Why is love a critical piece of sustaining God's revival in our lives?

- Is there a difference between telling someone "you are what you do" and telling someone "you should do what you are"? Is it the same or different? How does this affect how you correct others or yourself?

APPLYING WHAT YOU HAVE LEARNED

Now, what do I do?

- In what ways can you begin to sow in the Spirit actively? How can you apply Paul's statement to Philemon, "acknowledge every good thing which is in you" (verse 6) as a way of sowing to your Spirit and not to your flesh?

- How can you make "what God has done for you in Christ" the reason for all your actions? How will this motivate you to love others, pray, or be active in ministry?

- Knowing that you are the temple of God, that the Trinity dwells in you right now, that you are holy and blameless before God in love—how should you live your life? Knowing that rivers of living waters flow out of your belly, how should you interact with people?

www.ingramcontent.com/pod-product-compliance
Lightning Source LLC
Chambersburg PA
CBHW020534080526
44583CB00013B/860